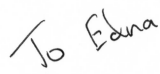

To Edna

Courage and Integrity

Jason

~Comments about the book_____

Interrogation of Morals

The Truth about
Courage and Integrity

By

Capt. Jason Meszaros
U.S. Army Reserves

J.P. Hewitt Press
St. Michael, MN

All photos provided by Jason Meszaros.

Cover Photos
Panoramic: Ridgeline overlooking village where Roze Khan was killed.
Back Cover: Jason Meszaros at Al Farouk Training Camp

First printing: October 2008

ISBN
1-4404-3673-8 (pb)
978-0-615-31234-7 (hc)
978-0-557-05036-9 (hc)
978-1-4404-3673-4 (pb)

Printed in the United States of America

~Dedication_____

This book is dedicated to the soldiers who served in Afghanistan, the Global War On Terrorism, those who have suffered due to terrorist acts and to the many nameless contributors to this book.

Additionally, this book is dedicated to the many families, spouses and children of the courageous soldiers serving our country in war zones each and every day. It is a testament to the commitment and love of our country.

Finally it is dedicated to my wonderful wife, who has survived the multiple deployments I served and I truly admire her courage, commitment and conviction. I couldn't have survived without her.

"and ye shall know the truth, and the truth shall set you free."
-JOHN 8:32

~Security_____

Names have been changed in this book to protect the identities of the many soldiers, law enforcement and intelligence professionals still actively fighting the Global War on Terror.

~Author's Note_____

This is a work of nonfiction. Events, actions, experiences and their consequences have been retold as I remember them. Other members of my team and soldiers I served with may have a different recollection or memory of the events. This is my version and the truth as I remember it.

~Disclaimer_____

The views expressed in this book are representative of the author and the author alone. The views do not represent, in any way, the views of other members of the Armed Forces or official policy of the Department of Defense.

"I serve my country but I fight for the man next to me."
-Anonymous

Contents

Foreword

Military Intelligence Creed

I am a soldier first,
but an Intelligence Professional second to none.

With pride in my heritage, but focused on the future.
Performing the first task of an Army;
To find, know and never lose the enemy.

With a sense of urgency and of tenacity,
Professional and physical fitness.
And above all: Integrity--*for in Truth lies victory*.

Always at silent war while ready for a shooting war;
The silent warrior of the Army team.

I spent eight months in Afghanistan in 2004. During that time I had the distinct honor of working with some of the most courageous and honorable Americans I have ever met. Those men and women served in the Army, Navy, Air Force, Marines, CIA, DIA, Secret Service, DEA, FBI and many other alphabet agencies. I experienced some of the scariest moments of my life and yet the most memorable. Fear has a way of emblazoning events in the mind, like a burned on cattle brand. When my thoughts are not occupied by my wife and my daughter, my memories are often both haunted by and filled with satisfaction from the work that I was involved in while serving in Afghanistan.

I learned the values of *courage and integrity* in ways I had never experienced them before. I saw the horrors of war and I saw the true meaning of freedom reflected in the faces of the people I helped. I also saw the hatred burning in the eyes of the people who want to destroy everything that America stands for and that angered me. Being away from everything that I cherish and seeing firsthand how the rest of the world lives only made my appreciation grow for what we have and what we were fighting to preserve.

Most Americans have never left America and have never seen firsthand the hard lives that the majority of the world lives. It's heartbreaking at times and yet it makes me feel good to know that I live in America. I live in a country where my success is directly correlated to the level of hard work I am willing to endure, my personal ambitions and the education system that is part of America. In America you earn what you have. America was built on the premise that everyone has the opportunity to make themselves into whatever they want to be. That doesn't mean Americans should just be given whatever they want. They need to work hard and earn it. That's the beauty of freedom. I will always remember the time I spent serving my country and giving others in the world the gift of freedom, but I will never forget that I live in America where freedom is a right we are born with.

I can't say enough about the level of dedication, patriotism and honor that the men and women that I worked with displayed day after day, even in the worst of conditions. Those words - dedication, patriotism, honor - are heard on the news and in the media everyday when politicians throw them around and pat themselves on the back. I don't believe that most men and women in politics truly understand the meaning of patriotism, not unless they have served in the Armed

Forces. Serving in the military gives you a perspective that cannot be duplicated, and it can't be learned in school, by reading a book and most definitely not by serving in Congress. I truly believe that. Patriotism has been used as a political weapon on both sides of the aisle and it saddens me to see it being exploited on the evening news. I've been in combat zones under administrations from both sides of the aisle and the opposition party always plays politics to inhibit the ability of the administration.

I want this book to be an example of the hardships, the experiences, the courage, the integrity and the honor that our military stands for. The military is and always has been a part of this country and will forever be here to protect freedom and liberty in America.

Chapter 1
The Army Still Needs Me?

I can't explain the mixture of emotions that ran through my mind the day I opened the letter from the Department of the Army. The letter arrived in a large manila envelope and I knew exactly what it was before I even opened it. At least I thought I did. I had been through a false alarm about six months prior when I received a similar envelope advising me of my transfer from the Individual Ready Reserve (IRR) to an Individual Mobilization Augmentee (IMA) position with the 101st Airborne. I never actually spent any time with the 101st nor did I ever travel to Fort Campbell, Kentucky (known as the home of the Screaming Eagles) but it was an honor just to belong to such an historic unit. Bottom line, this was my first clue that I would be getting deployed at some point in the next year.

At the time I received 'the letter', I was working for Retek Inc. managing an Information Technology Department. I am a computer expert - some would say geek - in the civilian world. Not the most glamorous or exciting job but it paid well and I enjoyed the work. It was relatively easy, and I had been doing it for a while so I wasn't overly stressed about going to work every day. There is also a certain amount of satisfaction from being the 'go to' guy, the one everybody calls for help. Being needed is ego boosting.

My days were filled with software engineers complaining about the type of mouse they were using or how slow their computer was performing (nearly always because they had installed so much "open source" software on it). The days dragged on and on and the boredom was broken only by some long distracting hours of gaming. Yes, gaming on work time. It happens. When times were slow and things ran well, as they usually do when you are good at your job, we I.T. guys ended up with a lot of time on our hands. The dot com bubble was bursting and we all knew the good times would be replaced soon enough. It was only a matter of time before the cutbacks or RIF's (Reduction In Force) would take place.

The military doesn't have the pleasure of experiencing layoffs the way the civilian world does, but as I would soon find out, the Armed Forces does lose men, but in a different and much more tragic way.

I hadn't worn my uniform for more than three years and wondered if it would even fit. Little did I know that it wouldn't matter. I wouldn't be wearing it much over the next year. I had surgery on my rotator cuff in March 2002, so was I even fit for duty now? To find out, the Army sent me for a physical in early 2003 and declared that I was indeed fit to be deployed. *Great,* I thought. Not long after that, I received the letter moving me to the IMA slot. Coincidence? Something tells me 'no'.

My boss at Retek Inc. was a great guy and very understanding, although he didn't have much of a choice in the matter. He did everything possible to accommodate and support me. We had been through this before so it wasn't exactly new territory. In 1998 I had only worked at Retek for four months when I found out I was deploying to Bosnia. Five short months into my new job I was on a C130 flying from Fort Benning to Ramstein Airbase in Germany. I was deployed with my Psychological Operations Unit out of Minnesota. The unit was the only one of its kind in the entire Armed Forces with the specific mission of Psychological Operations on Enemy Prisoners of War.

Our mission in Bosnia was to 'influence the long term feelings and beliefs of the Bosnian, Croatian and Serbian people'. We had to convince the three ethnic groups, who had been at war with each other for centuries, to suddenly live in peace and harmony. Sound familiar? Kurds, Shia, and Sunni, maybe? I think this was the pre-season for the Army in the game of nation building. We started with Bosnia and moved to Kosovo shortly thereafter and a decade later we are rebuilding Afghanistan and Iraq. We could have taken on the same task in Somalia in 1993, but instead we walked away and let the country fall into a state of anarchy, and it still is today.

It's an odd feeling to be in a foreign country wondering whether or not the people actually want you there. In the case of Bosnia, I learned very quickly that what mattered was who you were talking to. The Bosnian Muslims loved having the Americans there to protect them. The Serbians, on the other hand, did not want us there. They had been the dominant power for many years and wanted to continue being in charge. We were preventing that. My Serbian interpreter told us that when the Americans leave, they will begin killing Muslims again. With that mindset in the world it is no surprise that Muslims feel targeted. I learned a lot during my tour in Bosnia. I experienced the first elections in the country. I remember that like it was yesterday. It was truly amazing to see how happy the people were to finally have their voice in the form of a vote. The same was true for Iraq, and I'm sure nobody will forget the purple fingers being shown to every camera in the country.

Freedom does matter and America does some noble things in the world. The gift of freedom, even though it might be delivered through the military, is nevertheless a great gift.

The US Army Counter-Insurgency manual outlines a very clear strategy for Psychological operations.

FMI 3-07.22

PSYCHOLOGICAL OPERATIONS

5-3. The mission of PSYOP is to influence the behavior of foreign target audiences to support US national objectives. PSYOP accomplishes this by conveying selected information and advising on actions that influence the emotions, motives, objective reasoning, and ultimately the behavior of foreign audiences. Behavioral change is at the root of the PSYOP mission. Although concerned with the mental processes of the target audience, it is the observable modification of target audience behavior that determines the mission success of PSYOP. Leaders and Soldiers must recognize that everything they do or choose not to do has a psychological impact.

5-4. PSYOP is an integral part of all counterinsurgency activities. They meet the specific requirements for each area and operation. Mission planning for PSYOP in counterinsurgency must be consistent with US and multinational objectives—military, economic, and political. PSYOP planners must be thoroughly familiar with all aspects of the HN environment in which PSYOP is employed. This includes the history, culture, economics, politics, regional influence, and other elements that affect the people in the HN.

5-5. Commanders must consider the psychological impact of military and nonmilitary courses of action. PSYOP emphasize assessing the potential threat to the HN and the United States. PSYOP support the achievement of national goals by specific target audiences. In counterinsurgency, specific PSYOP goals exist for the following target groups:

- ***Insurgents**. To create dissension, disorganization, low morale, subversion, and defection within insurgent* *forces. No single way exists to influence foreign targets deliberately. Planning stems from the viewpoint of those affected by a conflict. The HN's government needs national programs designed to influence and win insurgents over to its side.*

- *Civilian populace. To gain, preserve, and strengthen civilian support for the HN's government and its counterinsurgency programs.*
- *Military forces. To strengthen military support, with emphasis on building and maintaining the morale of these forces. The loyalty, discipline, and motivation of the forces are critical factors in combating an insurgency.*
- *Neutral elements. To gain the support of uncommitted foreign groups inside and outside the HN. Effective ways of gaining support are to reveal the subversive activities and to bring international pressure to bear on any external hostile power sponsoring the insurgency.*
- *External hostile powers. To convince them the insurgency will fail.*
- *Local government. To establish and maintain credibility.*

5-6. PSYOP can assist counterinsurgency by reaching the following goals:

- *Countering hostile propaganda.*
- *Improving popular support for the HN government.*
- *Discrediting the insurgent forces to neutral groups and the insurgents themselves.*
- *Projecting a favorable image of the HN government and the United States.*

- *Supporting defector programs.*
- *Providing close and continuous PSYOP support to CMO.*
- *Establishing HN command support of positive populace control and protection from insurgent activities.*
- *Informing the international community of HN and US intent and goodwill.*
- *Passing instructions to the HN populace.*
- *Developing HN PSYOP capabilities.*[1]

Winning the hearts and minds of the local populace is generally considered the broad mission of the Psychological Operations Forces (PSYOPS). What does that really mean? How do you win the hearts and minds of a foreign population that you know nothing about? It starts with a lot of research. PSYOP soldiers spend a lot time learning about the country, the local customs and traditions and the belief systems. The main role of a PSYOP soldier is to modify that belief system and ultimately the ideology of the population. As I talk with people about the wars in Iraq and Afghanistan, they often tell me that it is impossible to change the way people think.

If that were true, there would be no need for advertising or marketing firms. Big tobacco would never have lost the case for targeting children. PSYOP starts with the children as well. We target the messages to each specific generation and create an environment for people where they see a future and something they believe in. PSYOP is about providing hope for people in a country where they have lived through wars, hunger, flooding, and despair. This message of hope is what enables them to believe in and support the Allied Forces. When the local populace supports the allied forces the PSYOP mission has been won. It's hard to measure and quantify the results with specific numbers, but in many cases it becomes obvious that the United States forces are being supported by the populace.

ZAMBOANGA CITY, Philippines — The convoy was about to depart a free medical clinic when two pre-teen boys who spent their days picking through garbage ran up and told authorities about the suspicious looking rice sacks with wires sticking out that lay nearby.

In the convoy of Filipino soldiers, doctors and nurses were about 30 Americans who were participating in a civil affairs mission to spread goodwill in an area that had traditionally supported Muslim separatists.

The boys had seen a poster describing roadside bombs and remembered that there were rewards for those who tipped off authorities to their whereabouts.

The convoy was halted, the bombs rendered harmless, and the boys would receive about $4,000 each and a scholarship to finish school.

The poster the boys had seen were part of an information campaign designed by a U.S. Special Forces military information support team, better known as psychological operations. Civil affairs teams had organized the free clinic.

These two lesser known missions — designed to win the "hearts and minds" of local populations — are being increasingly recognized as an important tool for combating terrorism.

Defense Secretary Robert Gates expounded on the use of so-called "soft power" to achieve U.S. objectives. "One of the most important lessons from our experience in Iraq, Afghanistan, and elsewhere has been the decisive role reconstruction, development, and governance plays in any meaningful, long-term success," Gates said[2]

A PSYOP team is typically paired with a Civil Affairs team that allows them to have an even greater effect on the population. Civil Affairs teams will perform a multitude of missions to include medical treatment, setting up education systems, and construction of basic facilities. In a typical counter-insurgency scenario as the insurgents are destroying infrastructure and attacking or intimidating the local population the American soldiers are rebuilding. As the local populace sees the changes and improvements, they will begin to realize that the Americans are there to help them. In some cases the change is instantaneous and can happen within the first meeting. In other cases it can take multiple meetings over an extended period of time. In either case it is imperative to have a consistent, convincing and compelling message the target audience can relate to. The transformation does not have to be quick. It can take generations to truly enact change, but the end result is worthwhile. Having a stable and democratic society where people can get educated and that treats all citizens fairly and respectfully should be the goal of all civilized society. The transformation begins with a possibility and hope.

I learned many lessons during my time in Bosnia. While it was not what I would call "hard combat duty," since the place was very calm, it did have its share of trials for us. For one thing, we learned convoy operations like the backs of our hands. Driving a vehicle in a combat zone is not like driving back home. There are procedures that must be followed in order for the convoy to remain safe. If and when the convoy does get hit, how the team reacts can mean the difference between living and dying. Even the simplest incident such as a flat tire can be a stressful situation. Changing the tire in the middle of a firefight is much harder than being on the side of the freeway back home. Soldiers in a war zone don't have the luxury of calling AAA and waiting for the tow truck to arrive and change it for them. The soldiers immediately need to set up a secure perimeter and working fast is critical. The longer the convoy is stopped, the longer it is a stationary target. The worst thing that can happen to a convoy is to be stuck in the same spot for hours. The insurgents can and will find out the convoy is sitting still and it is only a matter of time before it gets attacked.

Communication is critical to operations in a combat zone. We learned to trust and use our radios which are one of the skills that the National Guard and Reserve forces tend to forget. It's easy to forget how to use the complicated military systems if you don't do it every day. I learned the importance of doing vehicle inspections before every mission. All of the mundane tasks that Reserve soldiers complain about having to do on a weekend drill are the tasks that come to life when you get deployed. Most of the guys had spent little time training how to guard a fence line or pull guard duty but when we got to Bosnia, every soldier, staff sergeant and below, was assigned those duties. It wasn't fun but it was what soldiers do. Every soldier is trained in basic combat skills and every soldier utilizes those skills in a war. Maybe not every day and maybe not all at once, but sooner or later those skills all come into play.

The typical analogy when fighting counter-insurgency is like a hand in a bucket. When a military unit attacks and then secures a city, the insurgents will run out or blend back into the population. It then becomes hard to identify the insurgents and actually capture them. They go to great lengths to look like everyone else. The higher the insurgent ranks in the chain of command, the harder it is to identify him. The insurgents also employ operational security very similar to the American troops, meaning they try to keep the enemy from figuring out what they are going to do. Obviously, if we can figure out their plans it makes it easier for us to disrupt or stop them. That leads me into disruption operations. When they have to scatter, they lose operational control until they can regroup. Our best hope, and a primary strategy against insurgents, is to keep consistently and repeatedly disrupting them until they give up. The military strategy is to keep them constantly off balance so they can't implement a steady flow of operations. If they can't communicate with each other, can't meet and plan, then they can't effectively carry out their attacks. In the case of Al Qaeda, the senior leadership is always safely sitting in another country, while they send others to their deaths. Additionally, Al Qaeda has the patience and long term mindset that they can out last the Americans just like they out lasted the Soviets. When the hand is removed from the bucket, in this case U.S. troops move out of that city, the insurgents flow back in. They have nothing to prevent them from setting up operations again once the Americans are gone. In Iraq this was the scenario that would play out over and over again until the troop surge and the Iraqi Army became strong enough to step in and leave troops in the cities once they were cleared.

Much like a law enforcement operation that is tracking organized crime, a counter-insurgency strategy can focus on identifying the lower level commanders in the hopes that they will lead you to the higher level commanders. Once the organizational structure is becoming apparent the strategy will be to begin eliminating the mid-level commanders, which will in turn also disrupt operations. Initially, as the commanders are eliminated, it will be easy for replacements to be found. Recruits will be eager to step up and be in charge. It takes them time to regain control, however, and most of the time they will not be immediately effective. The new commanders will develop their own strategies and want to run the operations as they see fit. In Iraq, this backfired because the local Al Qaeda groups began to terrorize the local Iraqis with scare tactics such as beheadings and executions and in the long run this only turns the local populace against Al Qaeda. Every time there is a change in command, it takes time for the insurgents to adapt to the new leadership. It only takes a short time for the American forces to identify this new commander and as soon as we do and we have gathered the intelligence for an operation, he will be eliminated. This cycle will continue and over time the roles of mid-level commanders will be harder and harder to fill. As the lower commanders that are in line for the position sees their mentors and trainers being consistently taken out, they will become wary of stepping into the higher level roles. They know that once they do it is only a matter of time before they too will be eliminated.

The counter-insurgency strategy when I served in Bosnia under the Clinton Administration was a simplified version of the strategy that is being employed today in Iraq and Afghanistan. The basic premise revolved around presence patrols which entailed driving convoys of Humvees through the streets so the local population knew that we were in the area and that they should remain peaceful and calm. This worked well in a country that knew it couldn't fight back against the military might of the United States.

The difference between Bosnia and Iraq was that in Iraq we were fighting an enemy that believed they could defeat anyone. The enemy, Al Qaeda, thought they had defeated the Soviet Union in Afghanistan and therefore could beat the United States.

Al Qaeda also knows that Americans do not have the stomach for a long drawn out war that involves a consistent body count: Not a high body count compared to other conflicts, but one that will grow over time as they continue to inflict incremental damage to our troops and our morale. The constant media barrage of a small number of soldiers being killed every day will wear on the American people. The fight at home is much harder to win than the fight in Iraq or Afghanistan. The United States military knows how to win this war but without the support of the country, the politicians and the citizens back home, we will not be victorious. Partisanship needs to be discarded in favor of unity and support of the troops needs to be at the forefront. The greatest threat to US Military success is the lack of support from the politicians back home. This lesson should have been learned after every major conflict but with new generations of politicians, the lesson is easily forgotten.

All the while the nation building operations are taking place. Nation building consists of building the infrastructure including water, sewer, electrical and communications. It entails building hospitals and schools that will help the local population. The local population may see the positive change at first but over time they will begin to recognize the positive impact that having American troops will have on their society.

One of the most prominent memories that I have is of the Brčko Arbitration agreement. The city of Brčko is on the northern border of Bosnia, Croatia and Serbia. All three factions were vying for power and the international authority was making a ruling on who would get to govern the city. The decision was to be kept secret until the day it was announced. The humorous aspect of the so-called secrecy was that everyone in the country knew that the city would be declared multi-ethnic and everyone told to play nicely with each other. The best part of the story was that my unit was tasked with translation and printing copies of the arbitration agreement. We knew days ahead of time the outcome of all the legal proceedings. We forced my interpreters to translate, eat and sleep in a locked room for days until it was finished. They were Bosnian citizens and we couldn't risk the decision getting leaked to the public. The joke was on us. The morning it was to be publicly announced every paper in the country had the headline "Brčko -Multi-Ethnic City." I had a stack of newspapers that even though they were written in Cyrillic it was plain to see what the headline was. I was making copies of the arbitration agreement (for the ambassador nonetheless) when a lieutenant colonel walked by and scolded me for making copies. He began to lecture me on the need to keep the agreement secret, but I just handed him the stack of newspapers I had under my arm. He looked at the headlines, then promptly shut up and walked away. That was probably one of his better decisions.

Chapter 2
Battles on the Homefront

As you can imagine, my wife, Karen, was not very happy with the orders I received. After all, I had been home for three and half years straight without being deployed. Why should that change now, after all this time? If they hadn't needed me for three and a half years, why did they need me now? It was difficult for her to understand, and even harder for me to explain.

I wasn't about to walk away from my commitment to serve my country. The orders arrived November 1, 2003. Within days my wife stopped speaking to me, which is the last thing you want when you know you will be gone for an entire year. I tried every angle to spin it into a positive light for her, but I'm sure she felt that I was choosing the military over her. No matter what I said I couldn't convince her that that wasn't the case. It wasn't about choices, it was about service and commitment.

I contacted the unit I was being assigned to and asked them what I would be doing. They offered me very limited information. Little did I know the veil of secrecy that the unit was under, and what they told me was very simplistic compared to what I actually worked on.

I was told that I would be working in the Washington, D.C. area with a task force doing analysis on Al Qaeda data and intel. That sounded pretty cool to me. The greatest chance of deployment, they told me, was that I might get sent down to Guantánamo Bay, Cuba for research purposes. That sounded cool, too. I had no idea the task force had people in Afghanistan and Iraq nor what they did in those countries.

Karen and I argued constantly about what decision to make. I had to make a choice between serving my country by fulfilling my commitment, or staying home with my wife. Bear in mind that this is post September 11. I was already feeling incredibly guilty for not volunteering for service immediately after the September 11 attacks.

Karen finally began to speak with me again, and once we were communicating I was able to convince her that at my age and rank as an intelligence officer, the Army would never be foolish enough to send me anywhere that was dangerous. Silly me.

To further complicate matters, I had been working a second job as a collegiate volleyball coach for the University of St. Thomas where I was also working on my Master of Business Administration degree. The team was ranked ninth in the country as a Division III college volleyball team and I was very proud of that fact. We had a playoff match against one of our rival schools to earn a berth into the National Tournament and we were a virtual shoe in. Nobody had come close to beating us in the conference and the team and coaches were incredibly confident that we would win. The day before the match, the girls could tell something was wrong. I didn't want to tell them at such a critical point in the season but I had been honest and up front with them the entire season already so I broke the news to them. It was an emotional conversation.

The next night I invited my mother, sister and niece to watch the match. The girls were visibly different and not focused on the game. They struggled throughout the match and ended up losing to a team that we had beaten multiple times that season. After the match, I was devastated and blamed myself for the loss. My mother could tell I was distressed and I had to break the news to her as well. I had to tell her that her "baby" was being called back to service in the Army. It was my mother who was strong and to my surprise it was my sister that was visibly shocked by the news. The stress of having her husband in Iraq and his unit already having suffered multiple casualties obviously played into the equation. Now her little brother would be heading off to fight as well.

In spite of it all, Karen and I left for Virginia the day after Thanksgiving 2003. The drive from St. Michael, Minnesota all the way to Virginia was a very long and depressing journey for us to make. We stopped in Indiana and spent the night in a hotel and then drove the rest of the way to Virginia, the car sometimes filled with anxiety. We were both nervous, I guess, about what this new assignment would mean for our lives, and the changes that were coming. We both know that the military never tells you everything.

We finally arrived very late in the evening, tired, bleary eyed, and I missed the exit for our hotel. I remember getting upset with her for "making" me miss the exit. Like it was all her fault. Of course, it was completely my mistake, but the stress of knowing that I was going to be gone for a year was incredible. I was excited and guilty for being excited, all at once.

After a rough, sleepless night, we arrived at a base in northern Virginia the next morning, where the orders had told me to report. I was actually rather anxious to check in and find out what I would be working on with the task force. Al Qaeda was obviously a big topic in the intelligence world since September 11 and I wanted to help out, to contribute any way I could.

The first challenge was just to get on base. I had my orders and my wife along (who didn't have orders) and that posed a problem. The Army runs on paperwork. Most of the bases around Washington, D.C. had very tight security now and frowned upon unauthorized personnel being let on base. Fortunately, I'd had the foresight to get her a new military ID card at Fort Snelling in Minnesota before we left, and we were able to prove that she belonged with me.

The second challenge was getting the vehicle on base. The security team at the main gate of the base required a vehicle registration in order to log the vehicle into the system. In Minnesota we are not required to carry that document in the vehicle as required by other states. I argued with the security personnel for over an hour and made phone calls to get something faxed, to no avail. Finally, I went back to my truck and found a copy of the registration I had tucked inside a folder in the glove compartment inadvertently the last time I had registered my truck. Lucky me.

We proceeded to the billeting office to find out where I would be staying, and the personnel at the front desk had no record of who I was. Big surprise. Rather than argue, since I had been doing that all morning, I decided to check in with the task force and see what they knew about accommodations. This was the Army that I remembered from being a young Private. The Army that frustrated me and seemed so inefficient and worthless. I was young back then and didn't understand the complexity of an organization the size of the US Army. After spending a few years working in corporate America, I was a bit more tolerant and understanding of the situation.

As I walked to the door of the trailer, I found myself being disappointed and very unimpressed by the surroundings. It was an extremely boring, plain-looking building with no markings, no unit insignia indicating who owned the building, no commander's name on a placard outside the door, nothing to make you say 'wow'. It was a non-descript container and I was betting my future on what might go on in inside. I could tell that Karen wasn't impressed either. Had I really come all this way, left a great job, a great home, and driven half way across the country for this? What a letdown.

Inside we were greeted by an Air Force tech sergeant who matter-of-factly handed me a stack of paperwork to fill out. More food for the always hungry monster.

I introduced Karen and myself by saying, "I'm Jason Meszaros and this is just my wife." Oops. I'm staying here for the next year and this is "just my wife?" Huge faux pas. I apologized and tried to back pedal, but the damage had already been done. Karen was upset, and rightly so, that I had just minimized her entire existence to "just the wife."

This deployment was affecting her just as much as it was me, maybe even more so. We were a family and we needed to be a team or we would end up like so many other military couples and be divorced before I returned to Minnesota.

My first question was, "What will I be doing with the task force?"

The response was, "Classified. You'll have to talk to someone in the warehouse."

I didn't realize what that meant until a week later. What did they mean by "the warehouse?" What have I been sent to do for my country? It wasn't until the next day when I met with the head of the intelligence section that I learned what the task force was all about.

But as I stood in the anonymous unmarked trailer, I asked the million dollar question.

"Where am I staying?" Maybe, I figured, if we could spend some quality time alone, and not in the truck, I could repair the damage done by my inconsiderate remark.

I was told that the task force had been assigned a bank of rooms in the old Basic Officer Quarters (the BOQ) and that was where we would stay. The room turned out to be a decent two-room apartment style suite with a sitting/TV room, a bedroom, and a private bath. The rooms were actually pretty nice but there was no chance we would forget where we were and what we were doing, and think we were on some kind of vacation. There was no doubt it was an Army facility, but it still beat most barracks I've ever stayed in.

We made the best of it and I did manage to put a repair patch on my marriage, at least for the moment.

Chapter 3
Criminal Investigation Task Force

I spent the first month of my tour safely in northern Virginia working in a trailer that was not cleared to the security level of the warehouse. The Army uses different levels of security access, which it assigns to facilities based on their assessment. Most people have heard of *secret* and *top secret* levels. I was in a trailer that only handled *secret* information. All of the *top secret* work was done in the über-secure warehouse that required special access to enter. I had been granted a *top secret* security clearance by the Department of Defense ten years earlier. I can only assume that the delay was due to my not having used my *top secret* clearance credentials for almost four years. While I was frustrated by the delay, I later realized that I am comforted that the Army takes such great measures to ensure the wrong people do not access critical information. Security is a critical issue and is imperative to the success and safety of our military.

In the meantime, I was advised to read as much as possible on Al Qaeda and the Taliban. In the first month, I spent many long hours sitting in Barnes & Noble reading books and doing open-source research. Of course, that was in addition to the time I spent inside the secret world of Army intelligence. In that first month I read dozens of books and was completely overwhelmed with knowledge about the terrorist groups operating throughout the world. I'd had no idea there were so many factions and sub-groups. After a while all of it sounded the same. I suspect that most of the Al Qaeda experts know each other and share the same information because it all seemed to be repetitive.

One of the major themes that came out of September 11 was the notion that the terrorist of the new millennium was much different than the terrorist of the 70's. Both practiced a radical form of Islam, but the new terrorists were highly educated. I have some issues with that concept. Within any major military-style organization, the senior level personnel tend to be trained and educated at a higher level. In the case of the September 11 hijackers, they all had to have some level of formal education to get into the flight training courses for the larger planes. They also had to have a reason to be in America. It is very widely known that they entered America legally and through proper channels. For the scope and level of that operation, they needed to have educated operatives. I believe that Al Qaeda could put together another cast of twenty to thirty educated personnel for another attack, but the vast majority of Al Qaeda fighters do not possess the same level of education as the September 11 hijackers. There are probably hundreds or maybe even a few thousand educated, Al Qaeda trained personnel in the world. The question is, how many of them are willing to sacrifice their lives? My assessment is that the educated leadership would rather send the uneducated zealots into battle for the sake of Allah rather than go themselves. They consider themselves more important to the organization than the rank and file 'soldiers', whom they consider disposable. How they square that and justify it within their religion, I don't know. In Christianity, every life is of equal value. Apparently not so in radical leadership of Islam.

The second theme to think about is if Al Qaeda sends all of the educated members into suicide attacks, they will eventually run out of smart people who can plan the attacks well enough to actually pull them off. Al Qaeda needs the uneducated zealots for cannon fodder. The war in Iraq has proven this theory time and again.

The training camps that were set up in Afghanistan preyed on the young, uneducated Islamic men that had few other options and little or no hope for any kind of decent future. Al Qaeda needs ground fighters as much as they need special mission (i.e. September 11) operatives and they use Islam as the recruiting tool. In most common suicide bombings the level of education is generally much lower, if they have any education at all. It is easy to inspire an impoverished young man with a lot of energy and no focus and no future into committing acts that an educated person would find irrational. Plenty of fighters were recruited to fight the Soviets during the 1980's, in Bosnia and Chechnya in the 1990's, and now in Iraq. The cycle is continuing and will be hard to break. It will, I believe, be broken by establishing a democratic society in the Middle East where the young men and women can become educated and can see a future for themselves.

Some of the most interesting research that I encountered was learning the history of Afghanistan. The only history I had learned prior to this was watching TV as a kid and knowing that the Soviets had invaded the country. I knew Al Qaeda had been based there because of the U.S. invasion after September 11, but I had been out of the Intel world for so long that I wasn't up to date enough to be considered an expert. That changed incredibly fast, and waiting for my security clearance to be updated became a blessing in disguise. I was forced to learn about the vast history of battles that had taken place on Afghanistan soil for centuries, from Genghis Khan to Alexander the Great, to the British in the 20th century and later the Soviets. Each and every time, the tribal culture of Afghanistan saved it from being completely conquered. Even as the Taliban were conquering Afghanistan in the 90's, the groups that fought back, now called the Northern Alliance, did so with a fierce tribal vengeance. My need to pass time became my time to educate myself on the war being fought. It was incredibly valuable time, well spent, and filled with revelation after revelation.

In my second week I was finally allowed into the warehouse for an introductory training class that gave me an overview of the directive of the task force and background on Al Qaeda. It was there I learned that the task force had conducted the investigations of John Walker Lindh, the American Taliban, and the Buffalo Six.[2] The task force had the responsibility of investigating high level Al Qaeda and Taliban.

The official directive of the task force was:

> *To conduct and exercise overall responsibility within the Department of Defense for all matters pertaining to the investigation of alleged war crimes and acts of terrorism committed against U.S. citizens, U.S. property or interests; used in judicial and adjudicative proceedings including litigation or in accordance with a court order; and reporting of statistical data to Department of Defense officials.[3]*

The mission, as I understood it at that time, was to evaluate all of the detainees being held at Guantánamo Bay and review the intelligence to see what could be used as evidence. The main focus of the HQ task force was to screen the detainees and determine who was actually a hard core Al Qaeda operative, who was a low- level fighter and who was a non-combatant that inadvertently got rounded up and shipped to Cuba. Some of the cases were relatively easy. Many of the early detainee cases that the task force sifted through were not Al Qaeda at all. Many of them had been shipped over to Guantánamo before they could even be positively screened and identified. It was frustrating because the Al Qaeda operatives knew the stories that would keep them from being identified and were very good at keeping a low profile. It definitely was not the most glamorous duty but it needed to be completed, especially with the human rights groups screaming that we had incarcerated a lot of innocent people. Some of them were innocent. Many of them were guilty. Some of the guilty ones fooled us into letting them go. The Al Qaeda operatives that were trainers and appeared in videos were easy to identify and link. The task force had copies of every Al Qaeda video that had been recovered in raids since day one of the invasion of Afghanistan. I personally viewed many of those videos and some of them were pretty gruesome.

Some of the videos were instructional videos on bomb making. Some of them were torture videos of captured Russians during the Soviet occupation. For Al Qaeda, this is the ultimate recruiting tool. For example, our media will pick up a story like these videos as they did with the Nick Berg beheading video and it will get turned into a media spectacle. Nick Berg was an American contractor captured in 2004 by Al Qaeda and subsequently beheaded. The beheading was videotaped by Al Qaeda and released on extremist web sites as a recruiting tool to encourage other young Muslims to come fight the Jihad against America. The American media picked up the video and it was subsequently shown all over the world within hours. That's like free advertising for them, but with an open society and an unfettered media, there's unfortunately little that can be done about it. Some of the videos I watched at the task force were Al Qaeda testing chemical and biological weapons on dogs. These were literally some of the most disturbing videos that I watched. Strangely, these videos were never shown by the media; perhaps out of some sensibility that cruelty to animals is more horrific than cruelty to humans.

In the second week of task force orientation, I was amazed at the level of knowledge and the professionalism of the people on the task force. The most impressive segment of training was presented by a Special Agent named Timmy O'Hara. He taught us the background of Al Qaeda, how Al Qaeda was formed and how Osama bin Laden was originally introduced to Ayman Al Zawahiri. That would be the partnership that would change the world. The only history of Al Qaeda I knew prior to this was what I had heard on TV and read on the internet. You can get a fair amount of the story, true, but it takes researching multiple sources and analyzing the information. As I said before, most of these guys (writers) know each other and most of the history is documented from the same sources. The parts that I didn't know and would learn throughout my time on the task force pertained to the training and recruitment. Al Qaeda was portrayed in the media as a highly educated cellular organization. They were cellular, but the highly educated part was suspect in my opinion. Al Qaeda needed the ground troops and focused on recruiting them. The "executive" team and the next couple tiers were highly educated and able to mastermind an attack such as September 11, but the bulk of the organization were just 'good' Muslims willing to be martyrs in the war against the West and the Jews.

The task force was very quick to point out the success that it had enjoyed thus far in the war on terror. They had successfully investigated the cases on John Walker Lindh and the Buffalo Six. They had set up a task force of hundreds of law enforcement and intelligence professionals within a few short months after September 11 and had begun the tedious process of weeding through the detainees captured in Afghanistan. On the wall in the main briefing room was a map that contained all of the notes John Walker Lindh had made during his interrogation.

Special Agent Larry P Jester, who I will call Special Agent Bob, was one of the first members of the task force and has since written articles and manuals regarding the training of members of the government on Al Qaeda structure. The Criminal Investigation Task Force (CITF) developed a 50-hour course to train people on the history of CITF, Al Qaeda, Islam, Intelligence and Law Enforcement techniques for interviewing, and conducting crime scene investigations.[4] I later had my own issues with Special Agent Bob in Afghanistan, which will be discussed in detail. For now, let's just say he's an intelligent and knowledgeable man who truly believes in the mission of the Global War on Terror, and leave it at that.

Chapter 4
Infamous Guantánamo Bay (GTMO)

We arrived at the airport early in the morning to fly down to Guantánamo Bay. My task force training was over, my security clearance was in order, and I was anxious to get to work. In fact I was in such a hurry, I forgot to pack my passport. Luckily I remembered to bring along a copy of my orders. At least that's the story I told everyone. Actually, being the computer jockey that I am, I jumped on a computer in the terminal and printed a copy about ten minutes before the flight took off. Sometimes being good at riding the internet pays off.

We flew on the small white government planes with "United States of America" emblazoned on the side. Just like on TV. At first glance I thought this was pretty cool until I realized how small those planes really are on the inside. We landed somewhere in the Caribbean to refuel and then finished the journey to Cuba.

When we landed, we were greeted by the Special Agent in Charge (SAC) of the task force in Guantánamo. He led us down to the western side of the bay and introduced us to the FBI Agent who would be chauffeuring us to the other side. We climbed into a big old boat with twin 250 HP motors on the back. That ride across the bay was the scariest part of my deployment thus far. We were flying through ten foot swells and the FBI agent just kept laughing at the rest of us clinging to the railing for our lives. I'm sure this was the highlight of his day, scaring the crap out of the new arrivals. I had pictured many frightening things that might happen to me during my deployment, but drowning off the coast of Cuba hadn't been among them!

Once we were safely back on dry land, the SAC drove us over to the HQ and introduced us to the rest of the team. I met the intelligence chief down there and we spent a few hours walking through the process of transferring intelligence from Cuba up to CITF HQ.

We had a nice dinner that night at a little restaurant on the island and I heard some pretty funny stories about the guys on the task force. Most of them have known each other for many years and have gotten to be good friends. Cuba is not a terribly large island, and GTMO is even smaller, so it's a pretty tight-knit group.

I was up bright and early the next morning and did my morning run on the same road that was featured in "A Few Good Men". It may not have actually been the exact same road, but for the sake of my story it was. HOOAH!

I was picked up after my run and driven down to the HQ to start the morning's work. It was really pretty monotonous work and I got bored with it rather quickly. Luckily for me I wasn't there to take over, I was there to understand the process and head back to DC. My counterpart could tell I was losing interest and gave me a tour of the island. It didn't take very long and I finally threw out the question that had been hanging in the air, unasked.

"Can you show me the prison?"

He said he didn't have time right then but we headed back to HQ and he hooked me up with a couple special agents to take me over and show me around. I was excited to actually be seeing the 'real deal', which is a separate facility from the military base.

As we pulled up to the prison it looked exactly as I had seen it on television. The chain link fence and concertina wire on top to prevent detainees from climbing over it was rather ominous to look at. It is much more foreboding that it appears on the small screen. All that was separating me from being inside the most famous prison in the world was a sally port, which is common to pretty much every prison. A sally port is a series of gates where you must enter through the first gate and it is locked before they open the second gate and allow you to move into the actual prison. As we entered through the sally port I felt like I was walking through history. This place was all over the news for a variety of reasons and I was heading through the gates of the infamous prison at Guantánamo Bay.

The first place they showed me was the interview booths. Depending on who you talk with, they are either interview booths or interrogation booths. Law enforcement calls them interview and intelligence calls them interrogation. They serve the same purpose and from my experience are used the same way. A prisoner is brought in and you spend a few hours questioning him. I saw no evidence of the loud music chambers or sleep deprivation areas or even any torture devices such as a battery with jumper cables. Nobody was strung up by their ankles and being electrocuted or beat with a rubber hose while I was there. Based on the news and the reports from the human rights groups like the ACLU, I expected that to be the norm. Instead, what I saw were some innocuous interrogation booths that had intelligence professionals or federal law enforcement sitting and having a conversation with detainees. I know that sounds very tame but that's what I saw. Most of the questioning was preplanned to a certain extent and yet flexible enough to account for a prisoner reaching his breaking point.

The breaking point is when he has been caught in a lie enough times, has emotionally given up from the relentless questioning about the same topics over and over or has been tricked into revealing information without even knowing it.

There are many techniques or approaches used by the Army in interrogation that range from playing on a detainees fear, ego, knowledge, lack of knowledge, good cop/bad cop, etc. The reality is that many of these same techniques are used by law enforcement at all levels. There are a few that fall outside the realm of the law enforcement and there are a few that other agencies use that fall outside the scope of the Army. At no point in my training as an intelligence professional and at no time in my work in Guantánamo and Afghanistan did I ever witness an intelligence professional strike a prisoner. I'm not naïve enough to deny that it happens and I can cite a personal example of a detainee being struck by an Afghan soldier but Army interrogators are not taught to abuse prisoners nor is it encouraged. There is no denying that some bad things have happened in Guantánamo, Bagram and Abu Ghraib. That should not be the basis for judging how the Army treats its prisoners. Most of the abuses were the result of a lack of leadership or determined focus on the basics. The number of abuses is minimal in comparison to the overall number of interrogations and prisoners that have been handled through the system. I'm by no means defending the abuses and even a single one needs to be pointed out but by the nature of sheer volume; it was bound to happen eventually. Let me say this, **_TORTURE is wrong_**. I personally feel that everybody has their own moral compass and it is important for each individual to know which way his or her compass points. In a war zone in the face of the enemy, it is easy to get lost. The beauty of America is that we recognize when our moral compass is pointing us in the wrong direction. Americans are taught to speak up when they see something wrong and escalate the situation to authorities. The US Army has made numerous mistakes throughout history but they are always self-correcting. When abuses began in Guantánamo, the Army recognized that what was happening was wrong and began to correct it. Some of those mistakes made their way to Afghanistan and Iraq before they were caught. Once the mistakes were identified, the Army made its best effort to correct the situation and hold accountable those people who had strayed. That is the power of America, and it is what makes us unique in the world. Every human makes mistakes, law enforcement and military included, but in America we admit our mistakes and correct them, unlike other regimes and governments that either hide their dirty laundry, or tell the rest of the world to mind their own business.

 In the eyes of the public and the human rights groups there is a definite disconnect on what constitutes abuse even though it is somewhat clearly defined. The professionals who operate in this environment each and every day know that you have to build rapport with the detainee and gain their trust rather than abusing them with physical torture. The moment you strike a detainee you lose all ability to ever have that prisoner trust you. There is a line that you cannot cross and once you cross it you cannot go back. My training was to never cross that line. There are other, more effective methods to get a prisoner to break down and tell you what they know.

My tour of the prison concluded with a conversation with the PSYOP commander for the prison. This especially interested me because I had spent three years in a PSYOP unit that specialized in psychological operations with prisoners of war. I found it ironic that I was trained in PSYOP operations with prisoners of war and even deployed with that unit to Bosnia and never used those skills. Now years later I find myself in a prison working on a law enforcement task force and putting those skills to good use. In a low intensity conflict, PSYOP is used to influence the long term beliefs and ideology of a community. In a time of war, it can be used in conjunction with interrogation to speed up the process of breaking a prisoner down. Using a poster that will tug at the emotions of a prisoner is one manipulative method that is commonly used. If the interviewer is questioning a prisoner and asking questions that tug at the heart strings to break them down, it is very easy to reinforce that line of questioning with a poster hanging on the wall behind the interviewer that the prisoner is constantly looking at. It can be strategically placed to the left or the right of the interviewer so if the detainee is unwilling to make eye contact his only other focal point is the poster that reinforces the questioning. It is constantly in his direct line of sight.

I had seen this subtle and passive technique used in many training exercises but never in real life. We had actually designed these posters on some of the training exercises and it was truly amazing to see the real world use of that training. It is absolutely amazing how well the correct poster placed in an interrogation room can affect the emotions of a detainee. Some people would call this "mental cruelty" but I don't see it that way. The poster merely plays on the emotions of the detainee and his own prejudices as they relate to the religion, family, and homeland.

For example, in the Middle East, family is a very important part of the culture. A poster that showed the progression of a young girl maturing into adulthood would evoke a very emotional response from the detainees. Knowing that they are missing their children growing up makes them miss their family even more, and makes them more willing to cooperate in order to get back home. Another example is a poster that exploits the Muslim Religious holidays of Ramadan. The Eid is the feast at the end of Ramadan and is an event that every devout Muslim looks forward to. With the level of religious fanaticism in the terrorists being held at Guantánamo Bay, this is extremely effective in breaking them down and making them more willing to cooperate. All of the usual law enforcement techniques are used as well. Good cop versus bad cop, the we-know-everything routine (your buddies turned you in and have already caved), etc. While all of those techniques work very well, the most effective technique is what I call the cheeseburger approach. Was this the "torture" I had heard about in the liberal media?

The cheeseburger approach was developed by an Army CID agent along with an AF OSI agent. The technique was discovered by accident one day as the guys were running late and ran through the drive thru at a fast food joint at Guantánamo (Yes, they are there!). They showed up for the interview with a few minutes to spare so they decided to eat their lunch in the booth. The prisoner was mistakenly brought in a few minutes early and subsequently had to endure watching the agents eat cheeseburgers right in front of him. He was hungry and sick of the food in the prison so he solicited a cheeseburger from them in return for some very valuable information. From that point on whenever the agents interviewed that detainee they brought him cheeseburgers from the McDonalds on base and he kept giving information. Incidentally, the information has proven very valuable to the War on Terror and I personally experienced the value of the information gathered from him. The information that this detainee provided saved my life and the lives of the unit I was working with in Afghanistan. This particular detainee happened to be the master bomb maker and trainer at Tarnak Farms Training camp outside of Kandahar. He created detailed maps of the camp showing where there were booby traps set up within the camp. As we performed a crime scene investigation of the camp for use in the military tribunals we used those maps as guides and were able to locate and disarm or, at a minimum, avoid the traps. He did all this while downing burgers and fries.

The reality of operations with detainees is that if you make them miss the life they had before they were captured, the more they want to get back to that life. If getting back to that life means telling the truth about being a terrorist then most of them will admit it. If they can get a luxury item, such as good food, they will answer questions. To keep it simple, if you make friends with them and build rapport with them they will trust you and feel more comfortable telling you more details about what they did, saw and learned. Once you cross the line of physical torture, it is extremely difficult to cross back and build rapport with any detainee. I credit the professionalism and experience of the law enforcement personnel with ensuring that we were not involved in any questionable activities.

Within any prison system there is always an organizational hierarchy of inmates. In my experience, it was no different in Guantánamo, Bagram, or Kandahar. As with all humans, even certain prisoners can have natural leadership abilities. There are leaders, followers, enablers, tough guys, and wimps, just like in society. In a prison system it is easier for the natural leaders to step up and get others to follow them that in the general population. They can get people, who are a 'captive audience', organized into groups and set up logistical systems for supplies, smuggling, stealing and intimidation of other prisoners (and guards if they can get away with it). In many cases there are competing groups or gangs within any given prison. It only takes watching a couple episodes of "Lockup" on MSNBC to figure that out but I saw it play out in real life with terrorists in the most infamous prison in the world.

For example, we had captured a senior level Taliban Officer and he had been in solitary confinement since he arrived in Bagram. The MP's mistakenly placed him in the general population cells and the result was extraordinary. General population cells are basically large cages where sizeable groups of prisoners are housed. They all have a small individual space with a sleeping mat and a few personal items. At the entrance to each large cell is a sally port and at the other end is a toilet. Within minutes of the man being placed in the cell, the rest of the prisoners began bowing down to him and giving him praise and deferential treatment. Since he was Taliban and not Al Qaeda he did not have the same training that the Al Qaeda operatives had. He had been trained in Kabul in a military school and later at the Military University. He was quickly removed but it was obvious that the rest of the prisoners had great respect for him and would have revolted on the spot had he wanted them to. As a side note, American soldiers would never, in similar circumstances, be so obvious as to indicate an officer among their midst.

Another example was a time when the CIA turned over roughly fifteen prisoners that they had been holding at an undisclosed location. They were some of the highest level Al Qaeda operatives that had been captured to date. At the time they were brought in, the number of prisoners at Bagram had grown to capacity so there was no room in solitary for some of the prisoners. The MP's were forced to place some of the prisoners in general population and this was where we saw some serious consequences. Within a few days, the Al Qaeda trained prisoners had organized each cell into groups or units that had a particular role. They orchestrated a prison riot within a week of arriving and eventually some of them would escape from the prison. I had the distinct pleasure of both observing and participating in interviews with a number of them and found it interesting how much different the Al Qaeda trained prisoners responded compared to the non Al Qaeda trained. To me, it was always obvious when I was in the presence of a senior Al Qaeda member. Their demeanor and organizational skills immediately give them away.

Once we left the prison and returned to the HQ building I received a phone call. It was the head of the Operations team back in the states asking me if I would be willing to volunteer for Afghanistan and work for the task force over there. I was confused because a contract intelligence analyst had volunteered and was assigned to go. Apparently, however, the contractor he worked for decided that they would not send any personnel into a combat zone. Therefore the task force needed someone from the military to go. I jumped at the chance and had no idea what I was getting myself into.

Chapter 5
Afghanistan Here I Come

I decided to take a few days leave and fly home for Valentine's Day before I headed out to Afghanistan. I surprised Karen by having my buddy, Francis, pick me up at the airport and drop me off at her flower shop. My wife and I had purchased the business in 2002 and that was now her fulltime occupation. The retail flower shop was run very well, was successful, and I was very proud of her for all she had accomplished. We had another emotional exchange as I told her that I had volunteered to go to Afghanistan with the task force. I phrased it in a way that made it sound like Afghanistan was a safe place.

"Honey, it could be a lot worse," I said. "I could be heading to Iraq."

I returned to Virginia a few days later and began to prepare for my journey. I had to get all my bags packed and make sure I had the right equipment. I was given a bunch of clothing that was not very military. I was a bit confused so I started asking the guys who had been over there. I soon found out that operating as a task force we didn't wear uniforms in country. They also advised me to stop shaving and begin growing my beard. I immediately had questions about what I had signed up for.

My travel companion was none other than Special Agent Timmy O'Hara. That's a good Italian name if I've ever heard one. He loved that joke. He always complained he didn't understand why people said it to him, but he really knew. He was too bright to not know so he played along. He had been in a Ranger Battalion as a private but broke his foot on a jump and ended up getting sent to a new unit.

O'Hara had a lot of stories about his time in the Army and in the few weeks we spent together I am fairly confident that I heard most of them.

At Ft. Benning we proceeded through the processing station with a couple hundred other soldiers, sailors, marines and civilians that were deploying to various hot spots around the world. We received training in a variety of areas from weapons qualification, dealing with local nationals, and even some minor overview of how to deal with prisoners. I found that rather humorous considering what we were going to do.

We spent our obligatory day at the Central Issuing Facility (CIF) where they hand out all the combat gear that you are supposed to need. As usual I was issued about a thousand items that I didn't need and I was told that I had to take it all. The supply clerk from the task force told me to take only a limited list of what they issue because we had all the equipment I would need already in Afghanistan. None of that mattered to CIF. CIF said take it all and they weren't about to let me walk away with anything less.

The next day was spent going through all of our legal documents and making sure that we had all our ducks in a row so we could get paid, etc. More importantly, we made sure we had a Last Will and Testament and that the proper beneficiary was designated on our life insurance forms. Having gone through the same exercise when I deployed to Bosnia, I didn't put much thought into this part. Maybe I should have.

Day three we traveled out to the firing range to qualify on our weapons. We had requested to receive M-4's but of course were issued M-16's. We even had the commander of the task force call down to have them reissue us M-4's, but we were stuck with the M-16's. That's the Army. So we qualified on M-16's. We went out to a basic training range to qualify and ended up following a class of new fresh privates. By that time O'Hara and I both had substantial growth on our faces, taking full advantage of our quasi civilian intelligence status, and we were wearing civilian clothes. The trainees apparently thought we were "special ops" guys. Far be it from us to disappoint them by telling them the truth. The admiration in their eyes was worth a month's pay. If they only knew what we were about to be up to our scruffy necks in.

At the range we ended up with a bunch of macho cavalry scouts that talked a ton of trash about how good they could shoot, how their rifle was their best friend and how manly they were. Before long there was a river of testosterone flowing on the range. The best part of the day, however, was when the ringleader of the group failed to qualify after bragging loudly that he wouldn't even need all of his rounds. Oddly enough, on his second try he took fully loaded magazines and still did not qualify. He claimed the targets were bad. On his third try he finally hit enough targets to qualify.

Maybe I shouldn't give him crap because it took me three tries as well, but then I hadn't fired an M-16 in four years, and I was using a rifle that I had never fired before in my life. I didn't talk smack though, I just let the ammo do the talking.

We had a couple days of additional training on the laws of war and ethics in combat. The same training the soldiers from Abu Ghraib claimed they did not get. Nobody leaves to go to a combat zone without getting that training, period. Their claim just doesn't hold water.

It was finally time for us to depart Ft. Benning and we stopped by the operations room to pick up our tickets. We had specifically requested that we travel together since we had the same mission and destination. When we got our tickets, we saw that I was slated to leave that night and O'Hara was scheduled for the next day. After hours of arguing and working with the ops crew, he finally got his ticket switched so we had the same travel itinerary. It was like pulling teeth, but sometimes, unlike the battles over equipment and weapons, we won out over the Army bureaucracy. Sometimes it's the small victories that are the most rewarding.

Off to Afghanistan.

Chapter 6
Germany, Turkey, Kyrgyzstan and Kandahar

By early March, we were booked to travel through Germany, which in my past experience meant arriving there and then waiting for a day or two for the next flight out. That was in a time when we weren't even at war, so I didn't know what to expect this time. With the Global War on Terror raging on two fronts, I figured there were sure to be flights departing every few hours. In our case, we were on the next flight out because the task force had travel priority. We could bump just about anyone we wanted with no questions asked. It was nice to have some pull after being jerked around so much at camp.

From Germany we flew into Turkey. I had no idea where we would land in Turkey until we arrived and I found out it was an American Air Force base. We spent a few hours hanging out and some of the guys, okay a lot of the guys, smoked several packs of cigarettes. After being away from the military and in the non-smoking corporate world, I had forgotten how many people in the Army smoke. With all the stress that military members endure, I can't fault any of them for smoking to relieve some of that stress. I used running as my outlet for stress in the Army, but to each his own.

Out of Turkey, we flew into Kyrgyzstan. That's the place, you may remember from the news coverage, where the Air Force captain disappeared in 2006. She was supposedly kidnapped while shopping and I never heard how that turned out. The media must have lost interest in the story.

We checked in and had to take our weapons to the armory to be secured during our stay there. We had no idea how long that would be. After taking care of that we decided to check on flights into Afghanistan and were told it would be days before we would be able to leave, even with our priority status and ability to bump people from flights. We found that much of a delay unacceptable and began to network with some Air Force guys who were preparing to head in to Afghanistan. They had a dedicated flight with a few open seats but were flying into Kandahar instead of Bagram. We decided that Kandahar was closer that Kyrgyzstan and we'd jump on with them. Once we were added to their manifest we thought it would be a good idea to ask how soon they were leaving. It just so happened they were heading out to take off in a few minutes. Now we had to scramble to get our bags thrown onto the cargo racks and then had to run over to the armory and check our weapons back out and get back to the flight line before they took off. Needless to say, it was a hectic few minutes but we made it and within an hour we were in the air again, this time heading toward Afghanistan.

We were greeted at the Kandahar airport by a pair of Special Agents who I will call Bill and Ted. Even though they were from our task force, I can't say I felt a warm reception, especially when they found out I was an "officer". That would soon change. It took me some time to earn their respect, but eventually I managed. I will admit now that we all became good friends and the differences in rank became irrelevant. I would trust those guys with my life. In fact, I did.

Chapter 7
Finally in Bagram

We spent a few days tooling around Kandahar trying to see what interesting sites there were to see before we decided to actually get on a flight up to Bagram Airbase. Bagram Airbase takes its name from the ancient city of Bagram, and is located in the Parvan Province of northeast Afghanistan, north of Kabul. The Airbase itself is a huge facility with three large aircraft hangars, a control tower, and numerous support buildings.

I guess we thought we should enjoy ourselves for a few days before the real work started. In Afghanistan, however, that was not to be.

We ended up taking a late evening flight since most of the pilots like to fly after dark when the Taliban fighters with ground to air missiles can't see them. As we approached for landing, the pilots went into the standard evasive combat flying mode and the maneuvers and violent loss of altitude nearly caused every one of us vomit. I remembered that tactic from Bosnia but I hadn't experienced it in a few years and man did it come back hard.

We were still shaking our heads and trying to regain our equilibrium when we were picked up at the airfield by Special Agent Alice. She was the Operations NCO for the task force in Afghanistan. I don't know how she accomplished it, but while we were in country we were the most pampered task force there, guaranteed. We had our own beds, showers, real toilets, bedrooms, satellite TV and a refrigerator, which is all unheard of luxury.

About a month into my time, Alice came in and announced that she had acquired a bigger TV for us and some living room furniture. She never revealed who her sources were or how she got it, and I don't care either, because I enjoyed having a leather couch to sit on while I was serving in Bagram. She even hooked us up with a barbeque grill behind the building where our office was located. We had a freezer filled with steaks, hamburgers and ribs that came from who knows where, so we threw lots of barbecues. That may sound like something that soldiers shouldn't be doing in a combat zone, but for us the gatherings were more than just barbeques. We used them as a networking tool and as a way to build rapport with other groups. Sort of like team building exercises. We invited the interrogators that were working in the prison so that we were well connected and could do our jobs better. We invited the CIA and the DIA. We invited the Special Forces contacts that we had. Everyone that could assist us on base ended up getting an invitation at some point. We were learning what women know instinctively. Not only does an Army run on its stomach, but the way to a man's heart takes that route too. Our 'working barbecues' turned out to be one of our best intelligence assets and we made some good friends too.

Even after realizing that her talents seemed to be unlimited, I was shocked when one day Alice came in and asked if anyone was interested in purchasing a Starbucks Barista machine for making lattes. An Air Force guy, she said, was leaving and wanted to sell it for $300. I threw in $100 and everyone else covered the rest. As primary stock-holder, that made me the official latte maker for the task force. That machine became another tool in our belt for connecting with the intelligence units on Bagram. The aromatic smells of freshly brewed coffee attracted people almost as well as a card game.

Some competitive character flaw in me wouldn't let Alice be the only one who provided for us. She functioned like a den mother to us with all the things she managed to acquire. So I sent an email to my own mother and asked her to send us a bread maker, and of course she was only too happy to do it. What a coup that was. That bread maker paired with a latte machine in a combat zone made us the hottest spot on Bagram. It also allowed us to have a foot in the door with all the other agencies, units, and even some of the civilians. We lured them in with our luxury items and sealed the deal with our ability to provide value when units went after high value targets (HVTs). We were there, it was one of our primary missions, to make sure that HVTs did not get released once they were captured and in order to do that we had to be there when the got captured. Thanks to our espresso, warm bread, and luxury furniture, we now had the connections to make that happen.

I replaced a staff sergeant who I will call SSG Bug. SSG Bug was a nice guy, but like many young soldiers he liked to talk. A lot. Not just talk, he liked to talk about himself and all the "cool things" he had done while serving in the Army. Most of his stories were actually pretty lame and so I tuned him out a lot. I did pay close attention, though, when he introduced me to his contacts from the various intelligence units located throughout Bagram. I was incredibly intrigued the day he introduced me to the CIA Bagram station chief who I will call Lawrence. I can't think of a better source of information than the CIA in a combat zone. I immediately decided I had to make friends with him and become integrated into the intelligence world. I did exactly that.

To this day I still consider Lawrence a great friend and when I am in Washington, DC I look him up. We shared some pretty hairy times and covered each other's back on more than one occasion, which gave him some better stories to tell. He was always invited to our barbeques and had he been a coffee drinker I would have made him a latte whenever he asked for one.

The downside to Bug was that he loved going outside the wire (off base) even though he was not officially allowed to do that. Those rule breaking habits were a large part of why the leadership did not trust him. I didn't know him well enough at that time to know why and he left soon after I arrived so I'll never know all the reasons. I am just grateful that I did not get put under the same restrictions that hampered him.

My first trip outside the wire was actually on a mission convoy with Bug. He was driving, O'Hara was shotgun and Timmy and I were in the back seat. As we pulled through the gate, Timmy gave me instructions to sit back to back with him so that we could cover both sides of the vehicle. I was impressed by the way the others handled themselves as we left Bagram for my first time, which was obviously not theirs. I got some quick schooling, but would soon learn even more. A couple of interrogators that we'd already worked with inside of the prison rode in the second vehicle behind us. We shared a lot of information with them and they were a tremendous asset to us. They had early access to every prisoner as they came in for a preliminary screening. I was able to learn a lot about each of the prisoners by reading through those initial screenings and then briefing the agents on the background of each prisoner.

As we drove down to Kabul for this meeting, I seriously thought this might be the morning that I was going to die. Outside of Bagram Airbase there is a small village with a street that you have to navigate in order to get to the main road. The village is always filled with activity. From the street vendors to the people on motorcycles and bicycles, they swarm and swirl around our vehicles like bees disturbed from their hive. It is extremely unnerving to drive slowly through the swarm without having any way to know who is a simple merchant and who is a bad guy. The more you look, the more it seems like everyone owns a weapon. It was commonplace to see men walking around with an AK-47 slung over their shoulders, even merchants who just want to protect themselves.

Once we had made it safely outside of the village the guys told me I could relax a bit and enjoy the rest of the ride. That wasn't likely, but I did take a deep breath, realizing that I had been holding my breath the whole time in anticipation of being shot.

We drove past the ever present rows of mud huts and into the heart of the Panjshir valley. This area had been the front line for the Taliban during the early days of the war and they got crushed by bombing raids on this land that we were right now driving through. I even saw an unexploded bomb sticking out of the ground, like some kind of strange memorial. It reminded me of the episode of Hogan's Heroes where the bomb landed in the camp and Col. Hogan had to disarm it. Apparently there was no Col. Hogan around here to disarm the bomb, so it just sat ominously, reflecting the sun.

I was also amazed by the Kuchi nomadic tribesman that lived in tents and herded their animals all over the country. There were even wild camels walking around that we stopped and took pictures of, but you never forget for a moment that this is a strange and violent place. I memorized the route as we drove. I tried to visualize each and every spot that might be a good place for an ambush. There were really only two or three places on the route that would have been really good ambush spots, but the road was now so well traveled that I began to doubt that one could be set up without being seen. Someone would call it in and within minutes Apache gunships with their overwhelming fire power would be there to take them out.

We traveled at a high rate of speed and never stayed behind anyone. We passed every slow vehicle on the road, which was how we were trained to drive. We never let ourselves get boxed in or slowed down. We were in control on the road. We were in constant contact with the trail vehicle and communicated when to pass and when not to. I had learned these driving techniques in Bosnia and that training came in incredibly handy now that I was in Afghanistan. This place was like Bosnia on crack and without the green hills. It was like driving in a video game. Kind of like Grand Theft Auto only the armed people walking down the road weren't animated make-believe thugs and drug dealers they were hardened mujahideen fighters who wouldn't hesitate to put a bullet into an American if they thought it was necessary. We tried our best to keep it from being easy or necessary.

Once we got closer to Kabul, the traffic got heavier. It was obvious we were entering a city even though it didn't look like much of one by American or European standards. I still felt as though we were driving in a bizarre third-world video game. We got boxed in at one point between a couple taxi cabs and went over the median into oncoming traffic to get around the slowdown. We weren't about to let ourselves get trapped and become targets. We had to go around a couple traffic circles to get to the embassy, which was our destination. The traffic circles are a bit unnerving as well and could easily be a place to hit an American vehicle. The vehicles that scared us the most were the taxis and the motorcycles. Taxis because there were so many of them and it was impossible to tell who was inside. We could have passed bin Laden riding in the cab next to us and we wouldn't have known it. Well maybe we would have seen him, since he's so tall, but my point is valid. With all the dust and dirty vehicle windows the taxi cabs are like unknown molecules bouncing around the streets with anonymous passengers. The motorcycles were dangerous because they very easily weave in and out of traffic and could pull up next to our vehicle without us knowing. Motorcycles had been used as vehicles of choice for suicide bombings throughout Afghanistan and we were always a little tentative when one came flying up beside us. We kept them in our sites and we were trained to look at their hands for a detonator. It sounds paranoid but without that attention to detail we would be an easy target. I had a good life I wanted to go home to and I wasn't about to let that happen.

Bug told one story that I will never forget. He described a team that pulled up next to a couple sitting in a small beat up Toyota and ended up stopped next to them. As they looked over to assess the vehicle's occupants as we always do, the female in the vehicle looked up and made eye contact with one of the soldiers. Within seconds the male in the vehicle began hitting her for just looking at us. They badly wanted to pull him out of that car and beat the crap out of him, or maybe put a bullet into him, but of course couldn't do either. The moral choice here was to either let the man get away with beating his wife, or risk going to jail for a war crime (shooting an unarmed civilian). They chose their own freedom and swallowed the anger. I still get nauseous when I think about those guys not being able to help her. I don't know if the story is true or just an urban legend but soldiers face those same types of decisions every day in combat zones around the world.

In all the excitement surrounding my first trip outside the wire and down to Kabul, I made a huge rookie mistake. Something that I had done a hundred times before in Bosnia, this time I forgot. I left the gate and never chambered a round. If we had been hit, I would have been screwed. It didn't dawn on me until we were almost into Kabul and I asked Timmy if he had a round chambered and he of course said,

"Yes." I quickly chambered a round and had to suffer through the team subsequently making fun of me, as they should have. When you make a mistake in that hostile environment, you put not just your own life in danger, but that of your team members. It was a mistake I never made again.

Bug had actually managed to make some great connections and he thought they were really cool, but he didn't exploit them. He probably did not know how to exploit them. Those connections to the CIA, FBI and the Special Forces units operating in Afghanistan were the key to getting on the big missions. We had the perfect value proposition and he didn't use it to get "invited" along.

Once I hit the ground, I knew exactly what I had to do. He gladly showed me around and took me along to all of the daily and weekly briefings that he attended. He thought the briefings were 'cool' (a word he used a lot) but he talked more about what he *thought* was going on than how to take advantage of the access. One of the briefings was about a new detainee that had been brought in and Bug was very proud of himself for determining that the guy was a suicide bomber. The guy had shaved his body from head to toe which is a telltale sign of being a suicide bomber. He must have thought he was the only one who picked up on that because he talked about it like it was his own unique theory and nobody else would have noticed.

As we attended those briefings, I grew tired of listening to Bug pontificate about how much he knew, but one day he finally said something that caught my attention. He mentioned a Taliban commander named Roze Khan. Roze Khan had been thought to be a low level thug in the early days of the war but as time went on, it became increasingly apparent that he had a lot more power than originally thought. I began to do a little research on my own and learned that he had been on the target list for more than two years. I thought to myself, *we need to get this guy, and quickly.*

The briefing officers talked a lot about enemy combatants, al Qaeda, and Taliban fighters that had been targeted for a long time. Old news. Gulbiddin Hekmatyr was a big name and he had been on the target list for months. In fact, he had been around for a long time in Afghanistan and had developed quite a following. At one point he was the Prime Minister that ruled the capital city of Kabul in 1993-1994 and then again in 1996. He even had his own terrorist group known as the Hezb e-islami, or the HIG for short. The interpreters told me that during one stretch of the Afghanistan Civil War he launched over 30,000 rockets into Kabul in less than a week. He did more damage in that one week than the Americans have done in the entire war, which is amazing when you think about it. The majority of our bombing was done in the mountains or the Panjshir Valley where the Taliban were foolish enough to make a stand. He was reportedly captured in September of 2006 but that report was later retracted and he has since released taped messages calling for more jihads against the United States in Afghanistan. He has tried to take credit for assisting Osama bin Laden with escaping from Tora Bora in December of 2001, but I know otherwise.

Mullah Dadullah was another Taliban commander whose most entertaining name kept coming up. He was considered a key strategic aide and planner to the reclusive Mullah Mohammed Omar. He was also known to have communication with Omar, who has long been rumored to be helping hide Osama bin Laden, on a regular basis and that raised his target level even more. If we captured him alive he may be able to lead us to Omar. That would be a tremendous success for the American forces but it wouldn't happen. Instead Mullah Dadullah was killed in Helmand Province in southern Afghanistan by coalition forces in May of 2007, so any intelligence he might have been able to divulge was lost.[6]

Bug would also introduce me to Ben Steinberg. He signed his name Benny "the Jew" Steinberg in the Talibar, one of the facilities down in Kabul. Nobody ever called him that but he thought it was funny to sign his name that way, probably because we were in a predominantly Muslim country. The Talibar was a small bar/recreation area in one of the safe houses in Kabul where everyone who passes through signs their name to the wall. The walls are also lined with weapons. There is every type and kind of weapon imaginable hung up on the walls. This militaristic décor beat the usual memorabilia displayed in any sports bar I'd ever visited in my hometown back in Minnesota. The few early interactions I had with Benny didn't seem to go very well. In fact, he actually had me kicked out of a meeting in the SCIF because he was talking to the Chief of Intelligence for the 25th Infantry Division about a mission the FBI could perform for the Army. We actually got our mission directives from the Secretary of Defense but Benny thought the FBI should be tasked with the mission of supporting the military operations along with law enforcement support. That train of thought didn't last very long.

While on a mission near Kandahar, Benny and his team got ambushed by the Taliban insurgents and a 3rd Special Forces soldier was killed. That soldier was Chief Warrant Officer Bruce Price[7], a Green Beret out of Ft. Bragg who was on his third deployment to Afghanistan. Most of the Green Berets I met had already been to Afghanistan multiple times by 2004. I remember heading down to Kabul to the airport where we picked Benny up to bring him back to Bagram Airbase. Even days later, he was still shaken up shortly after that he left the country. I still have the utmost respect for Benny and what he went through, and I believe the FBI has an incredibly tough mission to combat terrorism. After his departure we would work much closer with the FBI. The walls were broken down and we were able to partner with them rather than compete for the missions. We both knew what needed to be done and we also knew that there were so many operations going on we didn't need to fight over them. That was my one and only experience with turf wars in Afghanistan and it didn't last very long. Fortunately everyone finally realized that there is one turf - the war against the terrorists - and it's going to take all of us to fight it. There's plenty of work and action to go around.

The task force had one NCIS (Naval Criminal Investigative Service) agent stationed in Afghanistan at all times. The NCIS agent when I arrived in Afghanistan was Special Agent Rob. In addition to being an NCIS agent, he was also a retired sergeant major from the Army Reserve and he was closing in on his retirement from NCIS. I mean really closing in, because he retired less than six months after leaving Afghanistan. He was actually scheduled to leave about six weeks after I arrived. I became good friends with him in the short time I knew him because we ate breakfast together every day. I was getting up and running about four miles each morning at 0500 hours and by the time I returned and showered Rob was up and ready to head to breakfast. We grabbed the same table just about every morning, and I really enjoyed his company. On the wall behind the table where we sat hung a plaque commemorating a soldier named Steven Checo. Checo was an 82nd Airborne soldier who had been killed during Operation Anaconda. I was honored to eat breakfast under that plaque every morning and it was a perfect schedule for my first six weeks.

After leaving Afghanistan and retiring, Rob took a job with a subsidiary of Halliburton known as KBR, Inc., or Kellogg Brown & Root. He would find himself working for them in Iraq less than a year later, and I'd be willing to bet he was making a hell of a lot more money than he did while serving in the military.

The Army Criminal Investigative Division (CID) Agents that were on the task force were Lucky, Timmy and Tommy. Lucky was a straight-laced, by the book, and extremely knowledgeable agent. He had been an instructor at the Army CID School for years and I could see why. He really knew his investigation procedures.

Tommy was a skinny young guy from Kentucky. He used his heavy southern accent to his advantage when he was in the interview booth. Prisoners would think he was really stupid from the slow, drawling way he talked but he was far from stupid. Tommy was also a runner and had been all through college. He convinced me to go for a run with him one day around noon. Not the best idea. Noon in Afghanistan is usually pegging well over 100 degrees. Needless to say I didn't make it the full six miles. Six miles was the distance from our office down the main street, around the airfield, and back up the main street to our building. I thought he was crazy when he asked me to run it because right before deploying I hadn't been running very much. I was also a few pounds overweight when I got there. I knew I didn't look much like a runner, which is probably why he chose me to challenge. He won that one, but by the time I left Afghanistan I was running the loop rather easily and I had lost about twenty pounds.

Tommy liked to play practical jokes. One day he decided to set up Special Agent Bob's Microsoft Word program to automatically replace the word "I" with "when I was in the 82nd". Special Agent Bob could not figure out how to make it stop or change it back so for a while all of his interview reports said "When I was in the 82nd" over and over again. He finally got angry enough that he ordered Tommy to change it back. Another time Tommy pulled a fast one on Bill by changing his keyboard to type in Hungarian. I, of course, got blamed as the resident computer geek (who eventually fixed it) but Tommy finally came clean and admitted that he had forgotten how to change it back and was too embarrassed to admit it. I've never decided if I believed him or not.

Timmy was probably one of the craziest guys I have ever met. He used to quote movies and one his favorite quotes, repeated at weird and inappropriate moments, was from Austin Powers. It went something like this: "At the age of fourteen a Zoroastrian named Vilma ritualistically shaved my testicles. There really is nothing like a shorn scrotum... it's breathtaking- I highly suggest you try it." Timmy was the token junior high school guy who always made gay and masturbation jokes. When Timmy found out that I coached college volleyball he asked me if I could get the team to send me a "swimsuit" calendar. I promptly said "absolutely not!!!" There is someone just like him in every unit I have ever served in throughout my time in the Army. They are the arrested development, Peter Pan buffoons who make you laugh in spite of yourself, and never heard of the term 'politically correct'. Don't get me wrong though, Timmy was an incredible investigator and soldier.

We had four interpreters when I arrived: Sam, Norbert, Abe and Phil. All of them were very good at interpreting but I had my doubts about loyalty from day one, which is the biggest challenge we face with interpreters. I had heard good things about Sam and Abe from the task force in Virginia, so I wasn't so concerned about them. Phil was Pakistani and the other three interpreters did not trust him and I sensed that right from the start. I didn't know why but I sensed their distrust and I latched on to that. In retrospect, I shouldn't have because Phil, it turned out, was an excellent interpreter. The most disturbing thing about Phil was his need to shower five times a day. I know it is an Islamic ritual but five times a day? Norbert seemed to be a really nice guy at first, but he ended up being a thorn in my side. I found out later that he was a follower of Wahabbisim (an extreme form of Islam) and actually thought the Taliban did a good job of running the country. When I found that out I questioned how in the world he got a security clearance. Of course I never got a good answer.

Captain Mark Cutter was our legal representative when I arrived. He made sure that we were following proper procedures and evaluated our case files. As our legal representative, he was also a member of the board that voted on which prisoners got sent to Guantánamo. The board consisted of five groups that each had a vote and they determined which prisoners would be released, which ones would stay at Bagram and ultimately who would be sent to Guantánamo. Mark was an incredibly intelligent man and I think he was keenly aware of how smart he was, but I still had a lot of respect for him. When he left it was a pretty sad event. He gave us a heads up on his replacement and we didn't really know what to think about it. That replacement would show up a few weeks later. Mark was kind enough to send us a box of Dominican cigars. They were fabulous and I enjoyed smoking a large number of them, but I also used them to bribe people and build rapport. Every luxury item that we came across could be used to get us connected and better able to fulfill our mission. But then sometimes a cigar is just a cigar.

Finally, I met Chief. Chief was a Vietnam veteran who had been in the Army since before I was born. He looked the part too, straight out of central casting. He had been smoking since he was about ten years old and his lungs were so damaged he truly had a hard time breathing in more cigarette smoke at times. He kept at it though. And I didn't complain about his smoking. I knew Chief had a good head on his shoulders, was very experienced, and I truly respected him as a commander. Chief was a commander in a combat zone and it was imperative that he have the respect and the following of his team. Chief had that respect from his troops and definitely from me. I couldn't have asked to serve a better man during my tour in Afghanistan.

One of the first missions Chief gave me was to get involved with the special operations units on Bagram and get us integrated into their system. He outfitted me with a Memorandum of Understanding (MOU) and a PowerPoint presentation to show them so that I could sell our mission. We had the mandate of the Secretary of Defense but in Afghanistan that didn't hold a lot of water with the secretive units in the special operations world. You couldn't walk in and demand that they take you along on a mission. You had to earn their trust and allow them to *invite* you to work with them. Once you proved yourself or built rapport with them somehow it was a lot easier to get invited. In my case I made friends with the counter-intelligence team within the Combined Joint Special Operations Task Force (CJSOTF). I had worked in that area before and I knew I could talk the talk. I made a presentation to the entire intelligence group within CJSOTF and they liked the value proposition that we offered. We would collect evidence during the capture of High Value Targets and ensure that they would not get let out of the prison at Bagram on technicalities or due to lack of proper evidence. Too many times they had sacrificed and put themselves on the line only to have the prisoner released months later due to a lack of evidence. In the wake of Abu Ghraib and the scrutiny that all the prisons came under, they were letting prisoners go left and right. The liberal left and the media were having a field day. The glare of the media caused people to be let go to fight again, that it had taken our men months and years to capture.

It was disheartening to watch this happen and we were on the voting committee that determined if people should be allowed to be released or if they should be kept at Bagram. We also determined who would be transferred to Guantánamo. When I arrived, there hadn't been a transfer to Guantánamo in almost a year because everyone was so gun shy. That would change with some of the guys we would help capture and hopefully the Military Tribunals would convict.

During my tenure in Afghanistan I would estimate that at least a dozen people were eventually transferred out of Guantánamo and sent back to Afghanistan to resume their deadly ways. There were more than just those twelve but I specifically remember those released prisoners because they returned to the battle field. They had managed to fool the board at Guantánamo and get released and as predicted they still wanted to kill Americans. We had the connections to the Guantánamo databases that stored all the information about them so the local command leaned heavily on us to identify them. My computer skills became a commodity very much in demand in a world where people are trained to shoot, not to type. I knew how to put together an SQL statement that would pull up the information that we were looking for, and I filtered out the unwanted information. Most of the analysts can manage to get the information but they also get a mountain of stuff they don't want. They then have to sift through it to determine what is relevant and what is not. I did that with simple code. It made me a rock star intelligence guy very quickly.
As you can see from the following reports, it happened time and time again.

Detainees Returning to the Fight
We know of several former detainees from JTF-GTMO that
have rejoined the fight against coalition forces. We have been
able to identify at least ten by name. Press reporting indicates
al Qaida- linked militants recently kidnapped two Chinese
engineers and that former detainee Abdullah Mahsud, their
reputed leader, ordered the kidnapping.
(Fox News report October 12, 2004, Islamabad the News
October 20, 2004, Washington Post October 13, 2004).
Mahsud, now reputed to be a militant leader, claimed to be an
office clerk and driver for the Taliban from 1996 to 1998 or
1999. He consistently denied having any affiliation with al
Qaida. He also claimed to have received no weapons or
military training due to his handicap (an amputation resulting
from when he stepped on a land mine 10 years ago). He
claimed that after September 11, 2001 he was forcibly
conscripted by the Taliban military.

Another released detainee assassinated an Afghan judge.
Several former GTMO detainees have been killed in combat
with U.S. soldiers and Coalition forces.[8]

Another Report
FACT SHEET
Former GTMO Detainee Terrorism Trends A DIA report
dated May 12, 2008 cites the figure of 36 ex-GTMO men
"confirmed or suspected" of having returned to terrorism...
with Kuwaiti ex-detainee Abdallah Salih Al-Ajmi's
confirmation of suicide bombing in Iraq, the figure is 37.

The number of former Guantanamo Bay (GTMO) detainees confirmed or suspected of returning to terrorist activities is about 7 percent of those transferred from U.S. custody. The identified rate of reengagement over three years of tracking has remained relatively constant between 5 and 8 percent. General Trends

Of former detainees known or suspected of returning to terrorist activities, those transferred to Afghanistan and Pakistan generally have reengaged in local, tactical-level, anti-coalition activity. Alternately, those former detainees known or suspected of reengaging in terrorism who were transferred to Europe, the Middle East, and North Africa have more often reconnected with terrorist networks associated with transnational terrorist activity, usually the same networks they were associated with prior to capture. Those returning to the transnational networks are assessed as more likely to be involved in future major transnational acts of terrorism.

In most cases, the time lapse between release and subsequent indications of post-transfer terrorist activity is approximately a year and a half, with reporting of such activity often lagging actual events by months or even years. Upon return, many detainees are held for varying lengths of time ranging from less than 24 hours up to several years. Due to the reporting delay and a general lack of information regarding former detainees, additional former GTMO detainees are likely to have been involved in subsequent terrorist activities.

Former detainees have participated in terrorist activities ranging from small-scale attacks to transnational facilitation and attack planning. However, the former GTMO detainees known or suspected to have returned to terrorism represent a small proportion of the total transferred/released.
Open-Source Reporting Identifies Detainees Reengaging in Terrorism

Ibrahim Shafir Sen*: was transferred to Turkey in November 2003. In January 2008, Sen was arrested in Van, Turkey, and charged as the leader of an active al-Qaida cell.*

Ibrahim Bin Shakaran and Mohammed Bin Ahmad Mizouz*: were transferred to Morocco in July 2004. In September 2007, they were convicted for their post-release involvement in a terrorist network recruiting Moroccans to fight for Abu-Musab al-Zarqawi's al-Qaida in Iraq (AQI). Recruits were to receive weapons and explosives training in Algeria from the Salafist Group for Preaching and Combat, which has since become al-Qaida in the Lands of the Maghreb, before going to fight in Iraq or returning to Morocco as sleeper cells. The organizers of the group reportedly intended to create an al-Qaida-affiliated network in the Maghreb similar to AQI. According to testimony presented at the trial, Bin Shakaran had already recruited other jihadists when Moroccan authorities broke up the plot in November 2005. Bin Shakaran received a 10-year sentence for his role in the plot, while Mizouz received a two-year sentence.*

Abdullah Mahsud: *blew himself up to avoid capture by Pakistani forces in July 2007. According to a Pakistani government official, Mahsud directed a suicide attack in April 2007 that killed 31 people. After being transferred to Afghanistan in March 2004, Mahsud sought several media interviews and became well known for his attacks in Pakistan. In October 2004, he kidnapped two Chinese engineers and claimed responsibility for an Islamabad hotel bombing.*

Ruslan Anatolivich Odishev: *transferred to Russia in March 2004, was killed in a June 2007 gun battle with Russia's Federal Security Service. Russian authorities stated that Odijev had taken part in several terrorist acts including an October 2005 attack in the Caucasus region that killed and injured several police officers. Odijev was found with pistols, a grenade, and homemade explosive devices on his body.*

Ravil Shafeyavich Gumarov and Timur Ravilich Ishmurat: *were transferred to Russia in March 2004 and quickly released. Russian authorities arrested them in January 2005 for involvement in a gas line bombing. In May 2006 a Russian court convicted both, sentencing Gumarov to 13 years in prison and Ishmurat to 11 years.*

Mohammed Ismail: *was one of the "juveniles" released from GTMO in 2004. During a press interview after his release, he described the Americans saying, "They gave me* *a good time in Cuba. They were very nice to me, giving me English lessons." He concluded his interview saying he would have to find work once he finished visiting all his relatives. He was recaptured four months later in May 2004, participating in an attack on U.S. forces near Kandahar. At the time of his recapture, Ismail carried a letter confirming his status as a Taliban member in good standing.*

Maulvi Abdul Ghaffar: *was captured in early 2002 and held at GTMO for eight months. After his release, Ghaffar reportedly became the Taliban's regional commander in Uruzgan and Helmand provinces, carrying out attacks on U.S. and Afghan forces. On 25 September 2004, while planning an attack against Afghan police, Ghaffar and two of his men were killed in a raid by Afghan security forces.*

Yousef Muhammed Yaaqoub: *better known as Mullah Shazada, was released from GTMO in May 2003. Shazada quickly rejoined the Taliban as a commander in southern Afghanistan. In this role, his activities reportedly included the organization and execution of a jailbreak in Kandahar, and a nearly successful capture of the border town of Spin Boldak. Shazada was killed on 7 May 2004 fighting U.S. forces. His memorial in Quetta, Pakistan, drew many Taliban leaders wanted by U.S. forces. At the time of his release, there was no indication he was a member of any terrorist organization or posed a risk to U.S. or Allied interests.*

Mohammed Nayim Farouq: After his release from U.S. custody in July 2003, Farouq quickly renewed his association with Taliban and al-Qaida members and has since become re-involved in anti-coalition militant activity.
Abdul Rahman Noor: Noor was released in July of 2003, and has since participated in fighting against US forces near Kandahar. After his release, Noor was identified as the person in an October 7, 2001, video interview with al-Jazeerah TV network, wherein he is identified as the "deputy defense minister of the Taliban." In this interview, he described the defensive position of the mujahideen and claimed they had recently downed an airplane.

Abdallah Salih al-Ajmi: Was transferred to Kuwait in 2005 and subsequently conducted a suicide bombing attack in Mosul, Iraq in April 2008. Three suicide bombers struck in Mosul on April 26, 2008, killing 7 people. Al-Ajmi had returned to Kuwait following his release from Guantanamo Bay and traveled to Iraq via Syria. He was apparently living a productive life in Kuwait prior to his traveling to Iraq to be a suicide bomber. It is unknown what motivated him to leave Kuwait and go to Iraq. His family members were reportedly shocked to hear he had conducted a suicide bombing.[9]

One of those detainees, Mullah Shazada, was released from Guantánamo and I personally know that he came back to fight. Fortunately, he was killed within a few months of his release. We knew where he had been killed but we needed to verify that it was truly him. An FBI team that we had worked with was tasked with heading out to the site where he was rumored to be buried, dig up his body and take DNA samples to send back to the verify his identity. The DNA samples checked out and it was confirmed that he had in fact returned to the fight as so many of them did. It is dangerous to be naïve about these fighters; their mission is to the death and they do not give up. We need to have the resolve to match theirs.

The prison was literally about ten feet from the building we lived in. Our job meant talking with prisoners every day so it made sense for us to be so close but it was also a bit scary to know that on the other side of the wall was a terrorist who would love to cut my head off. At first it made sleeping difficult, like you didn't want to close your eyes. After a while, though, I just got used to it. We were literally sleeping with the enemy.

Our accommodations had to be some of the best in the country with the exception of President Karzai's palace. We had satellite TV, air conditioning, indoor toilets and showers with hot water. We had satellite TV and nice couches, thanks to Alice. I slept on a real bed with a real mattress and so did the rest of the task force. The downside was that we spent a fair amount of time outside the wire and didn't have nearly enough time to enjoy our lovely accommodations. I won't complain about them because I spent enough time out at the firebases to know the conditions the infantry guys lived in and I truly appreciated what we had. We were definitely a well funded task force.

On the other hand I think we earned the luxury each and every day we were there. We spent countless hours with smelly, angry prisoners and even more hours out searching for them. Making connections with locals to get information about their whereabouts and coordinating with other Intelligence personnel to ensure that we all had the latest information was also part of the mission. That was the only way to get these guys. It took a concentrated team effort to track them down and capture or kill them.

Inside the prison there was a small weight room in one of the back rooms tucked under a staircase. The first month I tried to go back there every day and lift weights. I soon realized that I was completely out of shape and needed to make running the focus. Tommy would solve that problem for me.

My second trip outside the wire was again to Kabul. This time it was not for a meeting or an introduction to someone who could be of value to me - it was a shopping trip. O'Hara wanted to purchase an authentic Afghan carpet to ship home. He had convinced the interpreters to take us down to one of the rug shops in Kabul. I thought the concept of the mission was incredibly stupid and risky. Why would we take our entire team down into Kabul and expose ourselves, just to carpet shop. I voiced my concern but was overruled and ended up being an extra gun on the trip.

As we drove through Kabul this time I paid close attention to the streets and the route we traveled. Bug would be leaving soon and I would need to be able to navigate on my own in a foreign city. This is not a city that I wanted to get lost in and wind up in a "bad" neighborhood.

I took pictures of the traffic jams and the lack of any traffic control. It was a free for all driving throughout the city. Our only saving grace was that our white Toyota Land Cruiser stuck out like a sore thumb and everyone moved over so we could pass. It also meant we were a highly visible target and I thought about that every time I left the wire. I liked to take the black Toyota pickup that we had because it blended into traffic much better but Alice claimed it was a "grenade catcher." Hey, I would rather drive a grenade catcher and be invisible than be in plain sight for every bad guy in Kabul to target.

The trip took us into the markets of Kabul and I had flashbacks to Bosnia. I had accompanied the 10th Mountain Division sergeant major on a trip into Tuzla on a similar carpet shopping mission one afternoon and I was amazed that when we arrived we dropped our body armor and walked the streets of Tuzla unprotected. That would not be the case here in Kabul.

The first stop on the shopping trip was a place right in the heart of the city. I was amazed to see the street vendors with freshly butchered chickens hanging from carts along the side of the road in 100+ degree heat. I wondered how these people ate the food without major cases of salmonella. We stopped on a side street in a very unsafe area, in my opinion and everyone piled out to bodyguard O'Hara so he could buy his carpets. Mark and I stood guard on the street as everyone else went into the carpet shop. I watched as a group of old men sat and drank tea and chattered away about the American soldiers that were standing not ten feet away. I knew they were talking about me but I couldn't understand a word they were saying. They seemed to be getting more and more agitated as I stood silently and watched them. I finally sent Mark in to tell everyone we needed to get the hell out of there before the shit hit the fan.

Our next stop was for Rob to buy some jewelry for his wife. Again I was relegated to guard duty as everyone else went shopping. Thankfully we had gone to a much better section of town and the people seemed very happy to have heavily armed American soldiers hanging out with them. Well armed, bearded, and with all of my body armor I hoped I looked intimidating. We looked like war fighters, not interrogators and I tried my best to keep a game face on so that passersby would not be tempted to mess with us.

To my surprise, a little girl no older than six or seven years old walked up to me with her father. As he nudged her forward she very quietly and politely said to me, *"Thank you for freeing our country."*

My heart skipped a beat. I was touched and at that moment I knew that we were in Afghanistan for a good reason. We were there to provide this little girl with a future. This was my first glimpse into which direction my moral compass was pointing. I had never experienced a moment that truly felt so good and I knew that we had to continue making the right decisions.

I'll never forget that little girl's face as long as I live. Her smile made up for a lot of the other moments when I had not been certain of my mission.

Chapter 8
NCIS and Navy JAG

Rob left Bagram only a few short weeks after I arrived. His replacement showed up without much fanfare a few days after he left and there was no transition between the two. Nate Johnson learned what he was tasked with doing by reading through a document written by a previous NCIS Agent who had filled the slot a year earlier. For what it's worth, at least I had Bug around to show me the ropes.

Nate Johnson was a former HUMINT and SIGINT intelligence professional who had been assigned to the 19th Special Forces Group for quite a few years. His abilities and connections made him a valuable asset to our mission and our success and it was no mystery why he had gotten the assignment. He could walk the walk and talk the talk because he knew what he was doing. When someone is so obviously good at their job nobody questions their abilities. Nate was one of those guys.

The downside to Nate, at least as far as I was concerned, was that he dubbed me *"Lunch Box"* as a call sign. In Bosnia I used the call sign "Butcher" and it sounded ominous and cool to me. There was a simple reason for the name but that didn't matter. I liked having a cool call sign. *"Lunch box"* just didn't cut it. Once he said it, though, I couldn't lose it. I was stuck as 'lunch box' for the rest of my tour. A butcher could intimidate someone; nobody was going to be afraid of a lunch box. Oh, well, I lived with it.

Within hours of his arrival I already saw that he wasn't going to take any crap from the rest of the team. Lucky immediately started in on him and he was quick to retaliate. Lucky wasn't used to that. I liked what I saw. As much as I liked Lucky, I didn't think he was delivering on the mission that we were sent to fulfill. I sensed immediately that Nate would be different. Lucky's view of our mission when I arrived was that if we never left the wire, and all we did was interrogate prisoners all day long, that would be enough. I disagreed. As we discussed the mission more I began to realize where his perception had been derived. He was clearly following marching orders from SA Bob. Bob had ordered Lucky to maintain control over Timmy and Tommy and closely guard when they left base and for what types of missions. Bob didn't believe that any new prisoners would be transferred to GTMO and therefore we weren't needed to collect evidence when they were captured. I strongly disagreed with that. There are still senior Al Qaeda personalities in Afghanistan and when we capture them we need to insure they do not get released.

I believed that we needed to be utilizing the intelligence that we had accumulated in our massive databases back in Virginia and cross referencing and sharing that information to drive the mission in Afghanistan. The liberal media had been promoting the idea that three years after the war had begun the intelligence coming out of Guantánamo was not worthwhile. I can attest to the opposite - we used that very intelligence *while I was in Afghanistan.* With the computer skills from my civilian position I was able to mine the data and glean useful information. We needed to get that information into the hands of the operators who needed it. Nate and I would deliver on that mission. We made an incredible team and I would trust him with my life.

Lieutenant Don Miller was our legal representation. To this day I find it hard to believe he was an actual lawyer but the Navy had accepted him as one so it must have been true. He was tall and muscular and looked more like a Navy SEAL than a lawyer. He became part of the early morning running group and we circled the airfield in a pack too many times to count.

Don and I hung out on a number of occasions at the community center tent during USO events. We went down one night for the Hooters show and stood in the very back of the place where we could barely make out the faces on the stage. But let's be honest. We weren't looking at their faces. The Hooters girls could have been coyote ugly and we would never have known. Another event we attended was when Vince Vaughn came to Bagram Airbase. They set up a tent with a huge movie screen inside and showed a bootleg copy of one of his movies. Can't even remember which one. I thought it was pretty ironic that I was with the lawyer for the Criminal Investigation Task Force watching a bootleg copy of a movie. The only thing better would have been having an FBI agent with us when the anti-piracy screen came up. Wait, he was there too. And as far as I know, no one got arrested. So much for protect and serve.

Vince didn't show up until almost 23:30 hours that night and took a seat in the back of the tent. The security detail kept everyone at a pretty safe distance and wouldn't let anyone close enough to talk to him. I decided to use my special operations disguise - a beard and civilian clothes - to my advantage. I asked one of the security guards if it was possible to meet him since we had business to take care of that night. He of course assumed I was hinting that we were going out on an undercover mission and immediately led me to Vaughn.

The actor came over and shook my hand and thanked me for my service. I told him we appreciated him making the trip over and it was a pleasure to meet him. Then I made a bold move. I presented him with a coin that I had purchased and brought with me from Langley. That's right, the CIA headquarters. The bearded guy in Afghanistan gave Vince Vaughn a CIA coin. His face lit up like a Christmas tree.

He was beaming and couldn't thank me enough. That made me feel pretty good. It was awesome to meet him.

When we weren't attending U.S.O. events or working, we used to play a lot of Ghost Recon while I was in Afghanistan. We played every couple nights using the cooperative setting and practiced some of our skills on the computer. It sounds lame but we had a lot of fun. We would have competitions to see who would have the most kills during missions. After a while we got good enough that we could set it to allow only one death during the mission. That meant that if you died then you were done and you had to wait until the rest of the team finished or was killed. It made the game more interesting and put some real life caution into people. We didn't play the game like a teenager who would be running around and not worrying about being killed because he knows he can re-spawn and start over during the round. We took that factor out and made it mean something to die. How ironic is that? It changes the way you play the game and it changes the dynamics of the teamwork in the game. We learned to use our snipers differently than we used the close quarter's players. We played the game like it was meant to be played.

One night we were in the middle of a session and Don had just killed me in a "friendly fire" incident. I threw a Nerf football across the room and hit him in the back of the head. He was furious, and his face turned bright red. I swear I could see steam coming out his ears. Without even hesitating, he grabbed the nasty water bottle he had been spitting his tobacco into and hurled it across the room at me. He barely missed me, but lucky for us the bottle didn't splatter all over the wall. It was hilarious and Don knew it. Immediately after his over-reaction he stopped for a second and then started laughing.

In the midst of our games we used to take turns killing Chief. He was an intense player and he hated dying. At various times throughout the round someone would sneak up behind him and silently kill him. The reaction was always the same - a slew of profanity streaming from his office. It was awesome.

If you ever wonder why guys in the military bond so tightly, it's not just because of the moments when your life is in danger or you're being shot at. It's hang out times when a little male bonding goes a long way, builds camaraderie, and forges bonds of trust that often last a lifetime.

Chapter 9
High Value Visitors

One of the most high value visitors we had was none other than the Director of Central Intelligence (DCI), George Tenet.

In what must have been his final trip to Afghanistan during his tenure as DCI, I had the distinct opportunity - via the relationship I had built with the Bagram Station Chief - to sit in on the briefing held during his visit.

A small and exclusive group of intelligence professionals plus every general in the country attended. As the generals entered the room ahead of Mr. Tenet they all shook our hands and introduced themselves. We remained the nameless bearded guys in the front row as our mission and identities were still secret. One of the generals commented as he shook my hand that he liked how I had "shaved my teeth and brushed my beard." To this day, I'm not sure what he meant.

The two people who briefed the DCI were from the 25th Infantry Division intelligence staff. They included a major who was known as a Jedi Knight in the intelligence world. He had been selected and attended a graduate level school specializing in intelligence. Graduates receive a Masters Degree upon completion and are worshipped in the intelligence world. The other briefer was the young female captain that he had taken under his wing. She was rumored to be on a short list to get selected to become a Jedi Knight.

The young captain was an extremely eloquent and articulate speaker and I could see why she was so highly regarded. At least until I heard her make the statement of the year.

She said to George Tenet, the DCI that, and I quote, "There is no more Al Qaeda left in Afghanistan."

The rationale, I suppose, was that when we captured fighters none of them would admit to being Al Qaeda, so technically Al Qaeda must no longer exist in Afghanistan. I guess at that point it was safe to say that Al Qaeda had transitioned to the central front in the war on terror: Iraq.

We also had another high value visitor. Task Force Commander Col. Britain Mallow came to visit in May. I can't say for sure why he made the trip to Afghanistan but I suspect it had something to do with getting a couple months of hazardous duty pay and getting the tax break for setting foot in a combat zone.

Sound strange? All it takes is one day on the ground in any given month in order to get the entire month as tax free. It's amazing how some of the Senior Officer/Enlisted visits coincide with the last day of the month and the first day of the next month. They can make six trips into a combat zone for a total of twelve days and get an entire year of tax free salary. It's one of the little known facts surrounding serving in the military during a war. Now don't get me wrong, I do not believe the law should change. Most of those senior personnel have spent enough time in combat zones getting to their current rank that they are now to deserve whatever breaks they can get! They have all dedicated their lives to defending and serving our country.

The commander discussed at length, with all of us, the ramifications of the prisoner abuse scandal that had occurred in Iraq. We knew and understood that if we saw, heard about, or committed an act that could be deemed as abuse that it was to be reported immediately. Nobody on the task force felt that abusing prisoners was the best way to get information out of them.

I found it extremely disappointing that we even had to have the conversation. All of the honor and integrity that was at the very core of the military and my beloved Intelligence branch was being tainted. I knew what I had been trained to do and I knew that we weren't trained to humiliate prisoners as the guards had done at Abu Ghraib. I was sickened by the pictures and I had a feeling that the repercussions would be enormous. I was definitely right. Every move we made was scrutinized and anything that looked out of the ordinary was investigated. In fact, that mind set ended up causing me no end of grief down the road.

As far as our mission, the commander gave us the green light to begin building the relationships with the special operations. We knew that if a high value target was captured the only way to ensure that he would get a fair trial was if we were on the mission. We could collect and document the evidence and provide a chain of custody or basically a paper trail for the evidence. The special operations world is a small closed community and it is tough to gain their trust without being able to talk the talk and walk the walk. Unless they knew and trusted you it was hard to get "invited" onto their missions. That's where Nate and I excelled. Both of us had come from special operations backgrounds, Nate more so than I. We knew how to build relationships with the teams and sell our ability and the value that we added to the process. Too many special operations soldiers had watched as someone that had been captured shooting at American soldiers was released because the evidence did not support holding the detainee any longer. We knew that the value we added gave them more than enough reason to bring us along.

Unbeknownst to the commander, Nate and I had begun building those relationships already. I had made a connection with the counter-intelligence team working for the Combined Joint Special Operations

Task Force (CJSOTF). A staff sergeant named Jeff Smith and a warrant officer named Patricia Jones. They became very good friends of mine and I traveled out to firebases with both of them to get connected with the Green Beret teams conducting the missions. A firebase or more accurately a Forward Operating Base or FOB is a remote base in the heart of Taliban country.

The first trip I took was with Staff Sergeant Smith and we flew down to one of the border firebases and met with his team there. We had a DIA civilian who I'll call CZ with us on the trip as well, whose main mission was to look for weapons of mass destruction. He was a chemical and biological weapons expert and very knowledgeable in his field. He had worked on teams in Iraq numerous times and man, he had stories to tell. Staff Sergeant Smith's team chief from the firebase met us at the airfield and gave us a ride up to our lodging. Lodging was someone else's word; camp would have been a better term. Lodge sounds kind of cozy, rustic, like a log cabin and a fireplace. This was my first trip to a firebase in Afghanistan and I didn't realize the rough and remote conditions these troops were living in. It reminded me of the Vietnam film footage of those remote firebases. We hadn't even settled in when the team chief told us that we were going out to the firing range with the Green Beret team that operated out of the base. They had a bunch of captured weapons and we were going to go out and shoot them.

We jumped into the vehicle they had acquired, which was an old jeep with a bullet hole square on the middle of the windshield. The story was that an Air Force captain took a round square in the middle of his chest plate. We drove out the back of the firebase to the base of the mountain where there was a huge dirt embankment. They had targets set up that they were shooting at but they weren't the usual military targets. They had a group of small colored circles in two rows of three each. In these shooting drills the team leader would call out colors or locations and you had to double tap the circle in that location. As soon as we walked up the master sergeant in charge started running us through some shooting drills. It was pretty exciting to get some firsthand training from Green Berets on how to shoot. There is so much history and folk lore that surrounds them that I felt really honored to be in their company. I think my ability to hit the targets multiplied in triple digit percentage points that day. They were very good at their job, but who would have expected anything less?

We fired grenade launchers and PKM machine guns and threw some grenades over the dirt wall and watched them explode. The guys even fired off an AT-4 for us. There's nothing on earth a bunch of guys likes better than blowing stuff up.

As we drove back to camp we passed a convoy of soldiers leaving base to go out on a mission. The convoy vehicles consisted entirely of old junky looking Toyota pickups full of bullet holes, and all the men in those vehicles had long beards and were dressed like Afghanis. I didn't bother to ask who they were or what they were doing or where they were going, but I had a pretty good idea. I suspected they were some of the soldiers who didn't officially exist. One example of soldiers who weren't really officially in Afghanistan was the Army Ranger Battalions. Their presence was kept very secretive and was only revealed when Pat Tillman was killed about a week earlier. These guys weren't rangers, so they had to be one of the more secretive teams in the black ops world. It would have been pointless to ask who they were - they wouldn't have told me if I had. The black ops teams were all over and I don't think they operated out of any one spot. I'm fairly confident that was by design so that the enemy would never know where they were getting hit from. Regardless of who they were, it was extremely intimidating to pass them on the road. I was just happy to be an American and know that I was on the same team as them. You don't want those guys for enemies.

The rest of that day we spent hanging out and talking with the Green Berets and I did a fair amount of selling the value proposition of taking a criminal investigator along on every mission. They seemed very interested. I called back to Bagram and checked in to make sure the team knew I was alive and then went to bed. It had been a big day and I was beat.

The next morning we woke up early and packed into the jeep. I didn't know what we were doing but we had been invited to go out on the mission with the Green Beret team that day. I was a bit concerned about going out in the jeep we were in but I didn't really have a choice. I hopped in the back with the guys and off we went. I hoped the piece of junk would hold up and get us back.

What they didn't tell me was that we were headed up into the same area where Pat Tillman had been killed the previous week. Pat Tillman was a professional football player who walked away from a multi-million dollar contract with the Arizona Cardinals and enlisted in the Army as an elite Army Ranger. I wasn't sure where that was but I knew it was deep into Taliban territory and rugged terrain. I thought to myself that these guys may just be messing with me and telling me that to get me all worked up. We drove out through the village and the guys pointed out the areas to be concerned about and to keep a close eye on. They had driven through this village dozens of times and each time it probably spooked them. It spooked me that day. As we drove farther out into the countryside I took a picture of a small boy who ran through a plush green field to get up by the road to wave to us. I joked with everyone that that picture was my ticket to being a National Geographic photographer. It turned out perfectly.

A few miles out we turned off the road and headed down what looked to be a dried up river bed. It was pretty common practice to use river beds as roads and that was evident by the multitude of vehicle tracks. I would learn later on in my tour of Afghanistan the hazards of traveling down river beds. We drove for hours climbing up through some of the most beautiful and remote mountains that I'd ever seen. I can't say that I enjoyed the scenery much, though, because I was so focused on watching every movement on the ridgeline as we moved further down into the valley. Eventually we stopped for a pee break and as we were standing outside of our vehicles looking for a likely spot to water the vegetation and waiting for the okay to move, a burst of AK 47 gunfire erupted from behind us. Everybody dove for cover and frantically began to scan the hills for where the gunfire had come from. A minute or so later we noticed one of the Green Berets laughing his ass off. The gunfire had been one of the Afghan soldiers in the back of the convoy test firing his weapon. The rest of the day they made fun of us for being so jumpy, but the truth was that some of them had hit the deck too. I wasn't about to talk smack to a bunch of Green Berets though, so we took their razzing and let it go, glad we could provide a little levity for the bad asses.

The convoy eventually split into two elements and the front half kept going through the valley and our back half started up a path to get over the ridgeline. Our vehicle didn't have a first gear and wheezed and sputtered getting up the steep road into the village. I honestly didn't think we would make it up and was mentally dreading the uphill hike we'd have to make on foot. We finally entered a small village on the far side of the ridge and pulled in, then quickly set up a perimeter. This was our destination for the next few hours.

We were greeted by the village elders and the children came out and began to swarm the soldiers. I thought of my friend O'Hara and wondered how freaked he would be if he were here in the middle of these remote mountains surrounded by children. No matter how friendly they seemed, we had to remember that this was Taliban country. We had to be alert and watch ourselves, not let down our guard. The concern with the children was valid. O'Hara had been on a mission with another team and been left by himself to guard the vehicles. He was left without a radio to contact the team if something went wrong and was basically by himself. The children in that village had swarmed him and inhibited his ability to maintain any type of situational awareness. Add in the fact that most local Afghani men carry rifles with them and he is alone and surrounded without knowing who is a friend or an enemy. The issue is more with mission planning than the children but it wasn't a good scenario nonetheless.

The next few hours were spent merely hanging out with the local villagers. I met more children that day than I could count. Only a few of them spoke English so the rest of them asked questions through those children. When you think about how remote this mountain village was, it is amazing that anyone would speak English. There was one boy, roughly twelve years old, and he seemed like a ringleader of sorts. His older brother turned out to be the teacher in the Madrassa in the village and his father was one of the village elders. That explained why the rest of the children gave him so much respect. That's how the culture works over here. It's very hierarchical.

Through the course of questioning the children, we covered everything from the Pashto words for boy, girl, man, rifle, tea, and so on and so on. It was draining talking to the children because they had so many questions and they were so excited to be able to talk to an American soldier. They loved having us there. This was very similar to my experience working in Bosnia and having the children come out to see the Americans. They were also excited to answer questions from American soldiers and they had no idea that they were giving us valuable intelligence. The children knew and saw everyone that came through the village. While the adults would be reluctant to answer questions regarding Taliban patrols that came through, the children just thought it was fun to answer questions from American soldiers. We learned a lot about the Taliban's movements that day.

We had a PSYOP and CA team working with us on this mission and they brought along a school supplies and clothing to give away for the village. The Green Berets typically brought them along for this very reason. It was easy to build rapport and establish a relationship with village elders when you brought gifts for the children. That relationship would save lives because it was critical to the collection of intelligence to have the local populace on your side. If they did not trust the American soldiers they wouldn't give us the valuable information that we later turned into intelligence. We could piece together information from several villages to determine if the same Taliban groups had passed through and we could establish movement patterns. For all the grief the intelligence world took for failing to prevent the September 11 attacks, I didn't see evidence of that here. We were collecting and escalating constantly so the HQ teams could do the analysis. That analysis is what drove operations. Those operations took out Taliban and Al Qaeda operatives.

The school children came out from their classroom and the older brother led them through singing songs to us. They showed us how they could count and all the things we take for granted here in America. The children had the chance to learn and they loved it. We had given them that opportunity; even way out here in the remote mountains of Afghanistan they had opportunity. After a few minutes of the children showing off what they had learned, the CA team stepped up and began to hand out clothing. They had jackets to hand out and the children loved getting them. One little boy knew exactly who the Chicago Bulls were. I didn't ask how he knew, but I made the assumption that these guys had been here before. The greatest commodity to the children out here, even more popular than the team jackets, was shoes. Once the shoes were pulled out of the boxes the children quickly got out of hand. The teacher had to step in and establish control again. They were so excited to get shoes because they had no other way to get them. It was amazing to see them so frantic to get what children in America take for granted.

In the meantime, a few of the Green Berets and a team of Afghani soldiers had taken off on a foot patrol over the ridgeline to provide over watch for the guys in the village. If the Taliban were going to hit us in the village it would be from the ridgeline. If we were already up there they would unknowingly walk right into a firefight with the best soldiers in the world. CZ went out on the patrol with them. He was a former marine and was in pretty good shape and thought it would a blast to patrol with a Special Forces team. He had no idea what he was in for. They advised him to drop his chest plate from his body armor so he could keep up. I would have kept mine and sucked it up.

The team took off up the ridgeline and the plan was that we would pick them up about four miles down the road. The terrain they moved through was some of the roughest terrain I had ever seen. What I couldn't see from the ground was the well traveled trails that the Taliban walked every day. I wanted to go on the patrol but I knew that I would be more valuable on the ground talking with the villagers. I was also apprehensive about hiking through the mountains of Afghanistan with a bunch of Green Berets, and feared I wouldn't be able to keep up.

The valley that we were in was the same valley where Pat Tillman had been killed. I actually heard the real story about what had happened to Pat Tillman within days of his death. I don't think the Army meant any malicious intent and I don't believe they tried to cover it up. I think they were trying to honor a great American hero and chose the wrong route to do so. The guys that were there knew what had happened but weren't allowed to talk about it. An investigation was opened and the soldiers were instructed not to talk about the incident until after the investigation was complete. The officers back in the rear who filled out the Silver Star Certificate probably had no idea until after it was submitted that it was wrong. Any way you look at it, the situation turned out to be a black eye for the Army. Unfortunately, in war, in any battle really, lines often get blurred - it's called the fog of war - and mistakes happen. Signals get crossed, everyone doesn't do what they're supposed to, and mistakes happen. The real tragedy is that we lost a true American hero that day and his loss was no less significant because of the way it happened.

Once we had picked up the patrol we headed back to base. It was a very successful mission and I felt a strong sense of accomplishment about being a part of it. And in spite of all the bad mojo and apprehension, no one got hurt.

We flew back to Bagram the next day and I relayed all the intelligence that we had gathered. It was met with a great enthusiasm.

The same day the commander left Afghanistan to visit the task force in Iraq, I traveled down to another remote firebase with CW2 Jones to meet with another Green Beret team from the 3rd Special Forces Group. The commander and I sat together in the airport and chatted about the mission. We talked about the importance of having our task force represented during the capture of high value targets. We knew we could add value to the operations and ensure that the targets that we captured would not be released.

I connected with another team of guys from the 3rd Special Forces Group at the firebase. Surprisingly, having a long beard made it easier to build rapport with other guys with long beards. I was greeted by some of the men from SEAL Team 6 at the airfield. Seal Team 6 is the Navy's elite Counter Terrorist (CT) team.

SEAL Team Six or Naval Special Warfare Development Group (NSWDG)

aka: Dev Group, DEVGRU
Formed: 1980
Headquarters: Dam Neck, Virginia, USA
The Naval Special Warfare Development Group, (known as SEAL Team SIX) based in Dam Neck, Virginia, is responsible for U.S. counterterrorist operations in the maritime environment. Its origin can be traced to the aftermath of the failed 1980 attempted to rescue American hostages at the Iranian Embassy (Operation Eagle Claw). Prior to this, the SEALs had already begun CT training, including all 12 platoons in SEAL Team One on the West Coast. On the East Coast elements of the SEAL Team Two had taken the issue one step farther. They formed a dedicated two-platoon group known as "MOB Six" (short for Mobility Six) in anticipation of a maritime scenario requiring a CT response and had begun training (including the development of advanced tactics such as "fast roping") to that end. Yet, as was the case with the US Army's initial CT unit - Blue Light - and Delta Force, only one group was needed and could be recognized as official. With the formal creation of SEAL Team Six (a name selected primarily to confuse Soviet intelligence as to the number of SEAL Teams in operation) in October 1980, MOB Six was demobilized. A

large number of members, however, including the former MOB Six commander, were asked to join the fledgling group. With prior experience from these operators, aggressive leadership, and an accelerated training program, SEAL Team Six was declared mission-ready just six months later.[10]

The greatest compliment I have ever received was presented to me that day at the airfield. They actually thought I was one of them! I think it was the beard and non-military appearance but I won't complain. I would never presume to say that I belonged in the same category of war fighter as the men serving in SEAL Team Six but, damn, it was a great honor to be mistaken *for* one of them *by* one of them. What a rush!

A high school classmate of mine had been a member of SEAL Team Six. I knew he was still a member but for some unknown reason I hesitated to ask these guys if they knew him. Maybe I didn't want to seem star struck. It's not that big a unit and they probably did know him, and in fact I would learn later that he was in Afghanistan that year. Had I asked we may have been able to have a High School reunion right there in a combat zone. Me "the wannabe reservist intel guy" and him the real deal. I regret to this day not finding out from those guys if he was there. He was killed on February 13, 2008 in a training accident. The loss of another true American hero.

I connected with the Green Berets based out of this camp and gave them the briefing on what we could do to help them. They were extremely receptive and actually wanted to get our assistance. Unfortunately we did not have the man power to ever follow up and give them that help.

The Provincial Reconstruction Team or PRT being run by a Civil Affairs team was doing some incredible work. The firebase happened to be near one of the towns where Al Qaeda had located a training camp prior to September 11 so there were some strong radical Islamic feelings and this team was bridging that gap through textbook Civil Affairs.

I shared a room with an Army major from the Civil Affairs team. Basically there wasn't anywhere else for me to sleep so they threw an extra cot into his room. I didn't care as long as I had roof over my head, but he probably wasn't thrilled to have a roommate. I enjoyed a wonderful cigar my first night there up on the rooftop of the building. It was surreal moment for me, looking out over town. My time in country so far had been pretty exciting and had flown by very quickly.

The Civil Affairs team invited me to join them for a ceremony where they presented the police force of the city with a dozen motorcycles. They had a dozen shiny brand new little 125cc red motorcycles. The same little motorcycles that are seen in every third world country buzzing around villages, weaving in and out of traffic. As they were loading up the vehicles, I helped them get one of the motorcycles started. Apparently they had forgotten to fill them all up with gas the night before so they took a little finesse to get the engines fired up. I opted at the last minute not to go out with them because I heard I might be able to get a flight back to Bagram. The flight never happened and I was stranded for one more day.

I spent the time at the mobile hospital, set up to vaccinate the children in the surrounding villages. Local villagers would come to the base from miles around and were able to receive basic medical care. The children were given vaccinations and medicine as needed, and all sorts of ailments and illnesses were treated there. These efforts are one more example of the way that we are winning the hearts and minds of the local population through providing them with basic needs. Al Qaeda doesn't understand that. Their tactics of fear and intimidation work in the short run, but helping people is a much better long term strategy.

The 3rd Special Forces Group is headquartered out of Ft. Bragg and has been around since 1969. They normally have the mission of the Caribbean and western Africa. Since September 11, however, the Special Forces teams have been being deployed all over the world. Many of them have performed multiple tours in Afghanistan and executed large numbers of missions. They had the obvious mission of targeting Taliban and Al Qaeda fighters, but they also spent a lot of time training the Afghanistan Army. That mission bears a similar resemblance to the mission in Iraq. It takes training the local Army to protect themselves and the citizens before the Counter Insurgency Strategy can be successful.

HOST-NATION SECURITY FORCE OPERATIONS

3-36. The use of HN forces is essential to developing a stable society, one that looks to the HN government for long-term security. Whenever practicable, HN security forces operate in conjunction with US and multinational forces, and assume the major burden in operations when capable of so doing. The security forces in counterinsurgency consist of the civil police, paramilitary (also called the militia), and military. The elements of the security force work in concert to—

- o *Secure, protect, and separate the population from the insurgents.*
- o *Neutralize and defeat the insurgent forces.*

3-37. The first line of defense for the government is its police forces, which may be organized either locally or nationally. In either case, their action must be well coordinated with the overall counterinsurgency operations. The first objective of the police is to identify and destroy the illegal infrastructure of the insurgent organization. Police intelligence identifies and locates leaders, penetration agents, intelligence and propaganda agents, terrorists, and recruiters. The police arrest them using the minimum force necessary.[11]

In Afghanistan the training of the security forces had been left mainly to the Special Forces teams in the early years of the war. In Iraq that mission was originally focused on by the Special Forces teams as well, but due to the intensity of the insurgency that mission had to be expanded. That became in integral part of the mission General David Petraeus would implement in Iraq in 2007. That would be the turning point in the Iraq war. In Afghanistan, the mission of training the Afghanistan Army is critical to the success. On every mission I accompanied Green Berets on, we had Afghan soldiers with us.

Nate had already been in Afghanistan previously and a number of the guys he worked with on his previous trip were back in country. That made our ability to get "invited" onto missions much easier. He had instant rapport with them because they already knew and respected him.

A few weeks after I returned, I was sitting in the briefing room in the main Tactical Operations Center (TOC) waiting for the weekly intelligence briefing to start when I glanced down the row of chairs and recognized the man at the end of the row. He was none other than "Captain Alphabet" as his men called him. He was with the Psychological Operations unit that had replaced my unit in Bosnia five years earlier. I walked down and said hello and it took him a second to recognize me, again I suspect because of the beard I had grown. The last time he had seen me I was clean shaven and Army reg all the way. He immediately began ranting and raving, bragging about all of the incredibly valuable work that he had accomplished since the last time I had seen him. This was again one of those times I regretted being in the Army. Or rather, one of those people I regretted knowing in the Army. He liked to talk about himself and let everyone know how successful and important he was to the Army. During the course of his ramblings I learned that he was now the commander of the counter intelligence unit that was on base. He commanded the same unit to which Staff Sergeant Smith and Warrant Officer Jones belonged.

He proceeded to tell me how I had left Bosnia before the bombing campaign started in Kosovo and that his unit experienced all the crucial and dangerous work that had been completed in Bosnia. He patted himself on the back so many times during that conversation I was afraid I'd have to take him to sick call for a sling. I almost felt nauseous listening to him. He never once asked me what I had been up to. I kicked myself for not just keeping my eyes straight ahead and never connecting with him.

Later that day, I walked over to the Special Forces camp to talk with Staff Sergeant Smith about my conversation with Capt. Alphabet. I learned that day that some people never change. I heard the exact same complaints about his leadership style from Staff Sergeant Smith that I had heard from his men five years earlier. I only knew him for a period of two weeks back then but many of soldiers were already saying they were dreading spending an entire tour with him. That sentiment hadn't changed with his new unit.

I would later learn that Captain Alphabet had been passed over for Major for the third time. That might explain his obvious lack of self confidence, demonstrated through his ego-driven rants. Being passed over like that typically signifies the end of an Army officer's career, or at least any further rise in rank. The Army had made the right decision in my mind. The Army needs men and women who can focus on the mission and not personal glory. He liked his personal glory and he paid the price for it. In the military, the guys who only focus on themselves don't last long. They can only make it so far before somebody calls them on their BS and he had been found out. The Army, just like in corporate America, has its ways of weeding out the bad seeds. The Army is full of incredibly professional, honorable soldiers who operate as a team. Guys like Captain Alphabet should not be seen as the norm of the Army. They are the exception and they don't last.

Chapter 10
HQ teams

A team from HQ came to interview a group of newly captured high value prisoners that the CIA had just turned over. Many of them were linked to current investigations being conducted by the task force and were extremely important to the tribunals.

A few of our men were pretty upset that they weren't being allowed to do at least the initial interviews with these prisoners. Why did HQ have to send other agents to do the same thing we could do? The answer was that those agents were working on cases that these prisoners had intimate knowledge of.

My first experience with the high value prisoners was sitting in a meeting with the CIA and going through a PowerPoint presentation outlining the background of each prisoner. I remember distinctly how the CIA interrogator looked as he walked into the room. He had a little patch of hair on his chin and glasses like my dad wore back when he was in the Navy. Those were the early version of the BCG, or Birth Control Glasses, because when you wore them there was no way you would ever have sex. We spent a few hours going through the backgrounds and history of each and every prisoner. We learned who had direct contact with bin Laden, who knew about September 11 before it happened, and who had been involved in the planning of future attacks. These prisoners were facilitators. They moved money and people and made sure they got the training and support they needed to continue the war against the West and the Jews.

When bin Laden issued his fatwās, or declarations of war, in my opinion this is the group of jihadists that paid close attention. Bin

Laden might have been the one with the big vision, but these men had the knowledge and the means to make the attacks happen. It was comforting to know that they weren't getting out. They were locked up for a reason and that reason was because they wanted to kill us, not just soldiers but Americans and westerners in general. I could see the hatred in their eyes and hear it in their voices. That feeling of knowing that they would happily kill me in a heartbeat is something I will never forget.

We were given a briefing with an overview of the detainees by the actual interrogator who had been working with them since their capture. His name was Al and he looked exactly like you would picture an interrogator for the CIA. He had horned-rimmed glasses, was overweight and had the cheesy little soul patch under his lower lip. His knowledge of the detainees was fascinating. He had obviously spent many, many hours talking with them and learning about their operations and connections. I'm sure the ACLU and the news media would have you believe that most of the time spent with them he was hitting them with a rubber hose, blasting loud music at them, shooting them up with "truth serum" or even hooking them up to batteries. Of course that's ridiculous, or he would never have gotten the amount of information from them that he did. I personally suspect that he built up rapport and trust with the prisoners and probably used some sort of incentives to gain their trust and was able to get them to talk that way. It's a slow and tedious process but if you have the luxury of time, and we had lots of it with these guys, then you could usually break just about anyone without resorting to torture or even coercive methods.

The HQ team arrived at the airport and Bill picked them up and brought them back to the office. The minute he got back I ran out to help unload bags and get them settled in. I immediately said hello to Erika and Mary who I remembered from our flight down to Guantánamo Bay. They were polite but looked at me like they didn't recognize me. Then it dawned on me. We hadn't seen each other since February and I now had five months of beard growth on my face. I had also dropped about fifteen pounds and probably looked more like a mountain hunting guide than a soldier.

Erika finally said, "Jason? Is that you?"

"Yeah, it's me," I said, and laughed at her for not recognizing me. I think Mary was just scared of me at that point because she didn't say a word, just stared.

Annie was the next one out of the vehicle and I had never met her. She was a rail thin woman with long brown hair. It was much later when I found out why she was so thin. It turned out that she loved to run and the first day she went out for a run in Afghanistan she was stopped by the 25th Infantry Division Sergeant Major and scolded for wearing a tank top. We were in a Muslim country where the population frowns upon women showing any skin and there were a lot of local Afghanis working on base. She was pretty pissed off by that but succumbed to the pressure and wore a t-shirt for her runs after that. It's always been funny to me that when we're in other countries we adjust our behavior to their customs, but when they come to the U.S., they don't adjust to ours. I suppose it's because we are tolerant and respectful wherever we are, even when it doesn't go both ways.

Josh Carter was an intelligence analyst that had recently left the Army. He was now working as a civilian contractor for the task force and had served here in Afghanistan in the same position I was filling a year earlier. I believe he only spent about three months on his tour and things had changed quite a bit since he left. The one major factor that had not changed was that Roze Khan was still being hunted, just as he had been back then.

The group was actually a pretty enjoyable group to hang out with. They liked to play practical jokes and did things like launch "rock" attacks on our b-hut. The b-huts were basically plywood buildings with tin roofs and the yards were filled with fist sized rocks. They sometimes attacked our b-hut in the middle of the night by throwing rocks up on to our roof. The sound of the echoing tin inside the plywood walls was deafening. Another time the girls had sneaked into the b-hut and taken everyone's underwear and spread them all over the b-hut. Nate's underwear was on Tommy's pillow; Timmy's was, well, they may not have touched Timmy's for obvious reasons. The guys, of course, plotted their revenge. I stayed out of the games and was only a casual observer.

The payback came on the last night of their stay; the guys took some of the porn that they gathered from the b-hut and stashed it inside the girls' bags. All bags had to be emptied and searched when you left country so when they went through the customs inspection their porn would be discovered for all to see.

Josh Carter had become somewhat of an ass during the last couple days he was in Afghanistan, probably because he was not allowed to go out on a mission with us. His attitude and outward disdain for us warranted the going away present that he received. His tin of Kodiak tobacco was laced with eye drops which were "rumored" to cause diarrhea. The tainted tin was placed in the outside pocket of his carry-on bag and I can only assume he took a nice big dip to make the first eight hour leg of the flight home go by faster. The second little gift he was given was a tank sprocket. Yes, I said a tank sprocket, nice and heavy and illegal to take home. It was put into his duffle bag to make it over the weight limit and since we aren't allowed to take parts of foreign equipment home we knew it would be caught in the customs inspection along with the porn he now had in his bag. He would have a lot of explaining to do.

In spite of the hijinx, we worked hard, and quite frequently with the Document Exploitation or DOCEX team. They had the tedious but critical mission of sorting through documents that were captured on raids. They sorted through mountains of information, most of it worthless but some of it gold mines. I have to imagine they had one of the hardest, most boring jobs in the intelligence world. It was like being a treasure hunter and constantly thinking you had found something really cool only to discover that it was worthless. Every now and then you find something that is of tremendous value and it makes all the other unproductive time and effort worthwhile.

Chapter 11
Abu Ghraib and the Investigators

Once the Abu Ghraib scandal broke in the news, our lives became engulfed in the investigations, at least for the short time the media thought it was the hottest topic on the horizon. It was a huge distraction and seriously hindered our ability to perform our mission as required. We became security detail for the small task force that had been sent to Afghanistan to conduct prisoner abuse investigations. I and Navy Lieutenant Don Miller were tasked with this duty.

The small team of investigators that we were assigned to protect was tasked with inspecting and interviewing the field teams that held prisoners to determine if they had abused any prisoners. The inherent flaw in this plan was that nobody is going to just flat out admit that they smacked around a prisoner. The second flaw was the ambiguity of what constitutes abuse? The infamous memo that Secretary of Defense Donald Rumsfeld had signed, authorized the power to use interrogation techniques that had not been used before by the United States military. The memo gave the interrogators more leeway than they had ever been given before. This violated one of the ultimate checks in the system. The memo opened the door for the interrogators to make their own judgments about what constituted right and wrong and a few of them took advantage of the legal ambiguity. In an environment where the soldiers work long stressful hours, get little sleep and are dealing with some of the nastiest, most vile people in the world, it is easy to get bitter and lose sight of the mission purpose. It becomes easier to commit acts that would normally be deemed inappropriate. The compass begins to fail.

I witnessed a guard in the Bagram prison shortly after Abu Ghraib was exposed who began to taunt a prisoner. He was making the prisoner hold his arms straight out to his sides and was telling him how he was his favorite prisoner. I had seen this technique used before by the drill sergeants in my basic training class. Many consider this to be a stress position and therefore abuse. I disagree. If we are willing to allow our own soldiers to enforce discipline on each other with this technique then it should be appropriate to use on our enemy. Much of what goes on in colleges and passes for innocent hazing would probably be deemed torture by the ACLU, if they cared about college students. The counter to this is the argument that we are abusing our own soldiers. Again I disagree. I believe it is imperative to the success of the military to be able to use these techniques to train our soldiers. We have the best fighting force in the world and the tough rigorous training is what makes that possible.

I believe each of us has our own internal moral compass that forces us to decide which way personal moral decisions will go. It is very easy to get pulled into the wrong direction if we're not careful. Leadership needs to keep tight control of what the interrogation/military police teams are doing or they can lose their way very rapidly.

We were tasked with inspecting the holding cells that were used by all the Special Forces Teams at the firebases throughout Afghanistan.

Don and I spent a few days escorting the investigation teams around the country. We went to Qalat, Zormat and Ghazni just to name a few. It was really a boondoggle from my perspective because we wasted a number of days hanging out on remote firebases when we could have been actively working with prisoners or analyzing intelligence.

While we were at one of the firebases waiting around we sat through a combat lifesavers course. We just happened to be in the chow hall when a group of soldiers came in and started going through the training. We had been scavenging their food so we thought in order to blend in better it made sense for us to sit in on the training. A group of older bearded guys wearing civilian clothes blending into a group of twenty-something privates had me thinking we probably didn't blend very well at all. Since they stayed clear and asked us no questions, I can only imagine that they were a little intimidated by us. At least I like to tell myself that.

Don and I walked around the base after the class finished up and I saw something that really caught my attention. The unit that was assigned to this firebase as the security force was from my home state of Minnesota - the 34th Infantry Division - known as the Red Bull Division. The distinct Red Bull patch was proudly painted on the top of the gate, so I took a picture of myself standing under it and emailed it to my friends that were part of the Red Bull Division.

On the last day of escorting a Navy captain (the equivalent of an Army colonel), a Marine captain, and an NCIS agent from fire base to fire base, we had an unusual and amusing incident take place. The Navy captain was a squirrelly looking little guy with glasses. He looked like the guy who had been picked on throughout his childhood and became a lawyer to get back at all the bullies. We gave him an MP5 to shoot and it was scary to even let him hold a gun. He looked extremely awkward and it was actually humorous to watch him shoot. I'm not sure he even hit anything because the gun was nearly as big as he was.

We arrived in Ghazni early in the morning, thinking this would give us enough time to catch the Special Forces team before they left on the missions for that day. We were wrong, and found that they had left the day before. Only a handful of soldiers were left on the base. As the investigators interviewed the few soldiers that were there, Don and I watched movies in the break room they had set up. The family of one of the soldiers had mailed a DVD player, surround sound system, projector and screen for the guys to watch movies on. We took full advantage and took naps while 'watching'. At lunch time, we were enjoying an intermission and eating lunch with the NCO in charge of the fire base. We asked him if they had a shooting range we could use. Being a good soldier and loving any excuse to fire his weapon, he obliged us and took out to the range. He threw out some cans of Coke for us to shoot at which we promptly peppered full of holes and enjoyed watching the Coke fizz everywhere like a bunch of little kids. I'm sure we were a huge source of amusement to the Special Forces soldiers.

We all fired our rifles for a few minutes and then switched over to our handguns. I was shooting a Berretta 9mm, which is standard issue for an Army officer. We were all shooting the sniper target that was already sitting in the range. The target was a small square chuck of metal approximately 4x6 inches across and hanging down on chains. Every time we hit the target it would make the nice "ting" sound and swing back and forth. At one point in the shooting, everyone stopped firing to reload. I threw in a new magazine and started shooting again. I soon realized that I was the only one shooting and turned to see where everybody was, and saw only the Navy Captain jumping up and down behind me. Ignoring him, I promptly turned back around and began shooting at the target again. Apparently, the rounds were bouncing off the target and one of the shell jackets had hit the Navy Captain in the arm. As he was jumping up and down another ricochet managed to hit him in the leg. After the second round hit him I stopped firing and walked back to see what the fuss was about.

The first words out the captain's mouth were, "I'm hit! Do I get a Purple Heart?"

As soon as I heard that I walked back to the firing line and began shooting again. Maybe I could accommodate him.

The Green Berets drove him back to the main tent in the Humvee we had ridden out in and patched him up. They scanned his arm with a metal detecting wand to ensure they had removed all the metal. Once we had walked back to the tent and made sure he would survive his injuries we began to reload our magazines. As we were loading them up, one of the Green Berets came out of the medical room laughing about how funny the Captain looked. He told us that in all the time they had been stationed at that fire base they had never seen anybody hit by a ricochet from the target. They put thousands of rounds down that range and shot at that target on a daily basis. The amazing part was that the captain had not been hit once, but twice. I guess that can be my claim to fame. I can shoot a Navy Captain at 25 meters, bounce it off a target and hit him standing behind me, twice.

I'm not incredibly proud of that incident but it sure is one of the funniest things that happened while I was in Afghanistan.

A young Afghani boy waving at the American soldiers

Afghani boys

Outside the US Embassy

The vehicle we used

Bullet hole in windshield

Children receiving school supplies from a PSYOP team

The walk to Al Farouk Training Camp

The remains of the Mosque at Al Farouk

The team at Al Farouk Training Camp north of Kandahar

The staircase at Al Farouk

The obstacle course at Tarnak Farms near Kandahar

Randall, Nate and me

My seat for Operation Chargers

Roze Khan aka Taliban's Billy the Kid

Billy the Kid's Last Stand

Our ride home after getting Roze Khan

Lara Logan from 60 Minutes

Chapter 12
Interviewing and Torture

Shortly after I arrived in Afghanistan with O'Hara we learned that there was a high value prisoner being held in the Bagram Airbase prison. We were told a man named Arsala Khan had been transferred in from the CIA shortly before we arrived and nobody from the task force had been able to interview him yet. O'Hara and I volunteered. I wanted to watch the use of law enforcement techniques and see how and if they worked.

Earlier in my career I had been assigned to an Intelligence School at Ft. McCoy in Wisconsin. We trained soldiers in intelligence analysis, counter-intelligence, languages, and interrogation. I was given the title of Deputy Director of Training. I reported to a Lieutenant Colonel (LTC) who was a crusty old former tank operator who had transferred into the intelligence world years earlier. I got the feeling he regretted leaving the combat fighting teams for the intelligence world. I learned a lot from him during the time that he was my mentor. He forced me to sit through a number of training courses that were taught at the school knowing that it would prepare me for heading off to my officer basic course. The first summer I was assigned to the unit, I volunteered to spend the majority of the summer on active duty and spent just about every day sitting in a classroom learning the art of intelligence gathering. I liked to split my time between the analyst course and the counter-intelligence agent course. I never officially earned the Military Occupational Specialties or MOS because I hadn't completed my basic course yet and therefore wasn't eligible to get the additional designations, but I didn't care. I learned what I needed and that was what mattered to me.

At the beginning of my second summer the LTC announced that he was retiring. I was saddened by this and I thought I would end up spending my summer doing administrative work. I had volunteered to create a web site for the unit and I spent a fair amount of time working on that. Then my new boss arrived. He was a Captain who received his promotion to Major within weeks after arriving. I thought I had learned a lot from the LTC and boy was I surprised. The new Major spent more time mentoring me than the LTC ever had. He also sent me to the Battle Focused Instructor Training Course, so I was trained to be a military instructor. As a young 2nd Lieutenant that was unheard of. He tasked me with working with the interrogator instructors and learning the art of interrogation. I spent the rest of the summer working with them. That experience would be invaluable later in my career.

The instructors took me under their wings and ensured that I was involved in all of the activities for the course. I was featured as a guest instructor and taught map reading and some of the basic Army skills classes so they could justify having me in the classroom for the rest of the classes. I was an active participant in many of the role playing activities. Role playing is an incredibly effective way to train interrogators. I was given scripts to read and told to act in a certain way so that the interrogator-trainee would have to figure out which approach they should be using to break me. I learned every approach the Army uses by role playing the types of responses and behaviors that interrogators look for. I suspect I knew the interrogation techniques better than most of the students by the time the course was over.

Role playing was also used in the counter-intelligence course. I had the opportunity to work with that training course as well and learned the majority of the information that was taught, again through being a role player. One activity was called 'catch the rabbit'. I played the rabbit and we went to one of the local communities and I was to kill a day shopping, goofing off, and doing whatever I wanted. I would be tailed by a group of students from the class and they would need to remain unnoticed. It was easy to identify them the first time we ran through the exercise. They had been taught the techniques of blending into the environment in the classroom but had never put that to use so while they had the technical knowledge, they did not execute well. They would learn execution that day. We performed the same exercise a few weeks later with new rabbits and different teams and the results were dramatically improved. They had learned from their mistakes made on the first day and were indistinguishable from the local populace as the exercise progressed. Again, I had a lot of fun but more importantly I learned the fine art of surveillance.

By the time I headed off to my officer basic course I had already been trained in most of the aspects of being an intelligence officer. I was more than prepared and I breezed through the course without much effort. I left the unit after that summer because I had made a connection with a few soldiers from the class who were assigned to a PSYOP unit. I didn't know what that meant at the time but I put in paperwork to transfer and was in the new unit by October. I found out that the unit was the only unit in the Armed Forces that specialized in Psychological Operations and Interrogation of Enemy Prisoners of War. Everything was falling into place.

O'Hara and I decided that we would use a very soft approach with Arsala Khan's interrogation, at least to begin with. It would be easy to build rapport with a nice little old man, we decided. He looked like he was about ninety years old but he was probably closer to fifty. The Afghanistan sun and weather age people very rapidly, like tanning hides.

We spent many hours in the booth with him over the next couple weeks. We talked to him about his family and being a Muslim. We talked with him about the war with the Soviets. He had been a mujahideen fighter and told us quite a few very interesting stories regarding that time period.

We were extremely patient with him and finally decided to broach the subject of the American invasion in late 2001. We knew exactly where he had been captured and thought we could use that information against him. O'Hara and I brought in a number of pictures of senior Al Qaeda and Taliban members and tried to get him to identify those individuals. Our little plan was backfiring, because he told us he couldn't identify any of the pictures. We were baffled because we even brought in pictures of known associates that he should have identified without any issue.

Towards the end of the second week, O'Hara and I were both getting frustrated by the lack of progress. We knew it was a slow and methodical process to gain his trust and get him to open up to us and we were starting to question our abilities. O'Hara would be heading back to Washington, DC in a few days and we knew our timeline was shrinking. If we couldn't break him then O'Hara would need to travel back here again since he was the lead on this case. As we entered the booth on one of the final days of O'Hara's trip we noticed something about the little man. He kept squinting when we showed him pictures and still couldn't identify anyone, including a picture of himself! That was our last clue. This guy was nearly blind. We decided to take a chance. O'Hara was leaving in two days so we scheduled an appointment with the eye doctor for the next day. We drove the prisoner down to the hospital for an eye test. The eye test confirmed what we had suspected: he couldn't see a damn thing. The doctor gave us a prescription for him and we ordered a pair of glasses for the little man.

O'Hara left the next day and I was tasked with getting the glasses and making sure they did the job. It took us another month to get them but the results were incredible. We tried to have the hospital order them but they claimed they had to send the order back to the states and have the glasses shipped over. We couldn't wait that long so we decided to take matters into our own hands. We made a trip down to Kabul and had our interpreters order the glasses and have the prescription filled. As expected in Afghanistan, there are no one-hour eyeglass stores. It still took them a few days to fill the prescription but at least we had our key.

I sent O'Hara an email and asked him how he wanted us to proceed. He said grab one of the other Special Agents and present the man with the glasses. We went in that afternoon and let him try the glasses out. He was in heaven. We had given this poor little Afghani man the gift of sight. He hadn't been able to see anything for years and now everything was as clear as day. We didn't do a lot of questioning that day other than the usual small talk to get him excited. We told him we had to keep the glasses for now but that we would be bringing them back to him in a few weeks.

I emailed O'Hara and he was ecstatic to learn that the glasses had worked. He said he would schedule another trip to Afghanistan in the next week and we could resume our questioning. That, unfortunately, wouldn't happen. O'Hara got denied the trip and was told he was needed back in Washington. I had begun to get integrated into the Special Operations units by that time and would not follow up with the prisoner either. It was looking like some other team would benefit from our hard work and innovative solution.

It took almost three months before O'Hara was able to return to Afghanistan and I wasn't sure the prisoner would even remember us.

When O'Hara finally arrived, we were both excited to get back in the booth with the prisoner, but the delays kept coming. We would have to wait for one more day. Finally we sat down in the booth armed with the glasses, a stack of pictures, and a map. We thought this interview would be a quick in and out but it turned into an all day event for us. As we gave him back the glasses, he became overwhelmed with emotion and broke down into tears. He could not believe that someone would care so much about him that we would give him glasses. Of course our intentions were not purely charitable; we did have an ulterior motive, but it was fine with us that he thought we were great guys.

Once the questioning started, he opened up very quickly. We had taken the time and effort to build the rapport and the trust necessary to get a prisoner to tell us whatever we asked him. We began to show him pictures and he immediately started to identify senior level Al Qaeda and Taliban personalities. Our method had worked. He even identified Osama bin Laden himself as the "tall Arab" he had led out of Tora Bora in December of 2001. He confirmed what had been suspected all along. He identified routes on a map and we plotted the exact route he had taken to get into Pakistan. It was amazing to witness the level of trust that he had for us.

In the wake of Abu Ghraib and Guantánamo Bay, it would seem from press reports that prisoner torture was a common place practice. I strongly disagree with that erroneous perception. My experience reflects a very professional and methodical world of intelligence collection. I did not witness the torture as portrayed in the movies or by Hollywood or even in the liberal media. In real life, the interrogation of prisoners does not take place as perceived by media and therefore wrongly communicated to the American public. I won't deny that there are a few rogue elements that have watched too many movies and therefore try to use techniques they think are cool. Trained and experienced interrogators understand that those heavy-handed techniques rarely work and are employed by true intelligence professionals in only the most extreme circumstances, such as when an imminent threat is suspected and lives may be lost. Few people know that while from press reports and naïve liberals one would think that water boarding is a widespread practice, there have only been three - yes, three - instances where that was used, and those were very bad guys concealing knowledge about imminent threats. Lives were saved.

The military police that teased and harassed the prisoners at Abu Ghraib were wrong and deserved to be punished. The commanders who authorized the use of those techniques deserved to be punished. And that's the beauty of the American system - a wrong was committed and the wrong-doers were punished. When we see something that is wrong we take measures to correct it and adjust our behavior. The same cannot be said for our enemies and we must hold ourselves to a higher moral standard and punish those who break our moral and ethical code. Our system does work.

The biggest revelation that came out of our interrogations of the prisoner was from O'Hara. He was convinced that we knew where bin Laden was hiding and we could go capture him that day. The rest of us disagreed knowing that Bin Laden moved daily and never spent more than a few hours in the same spot. It was crazy to think he was hiding in a cave that this little old man said he was in. The truth be told, I actually agreed with O'Hara to some extent. I knew that Bin

Laden felt safe and secure in the mountains being harbored by the loyal villagers. I am confident that he has a pretty specific route that he follows and spends time in the same villages repeatedly. His movements are probably random but he has a comfort zone that he is not willing to leave. There is too much risk for him of revealing his position if he ventures outside of that area. O'Hara and I believed that if we could identify some of those safes areas it might prove to be the key to capturing him. This one elderly prisoner might hold the key in his shaky grasp. But it was not to be. We would not accomplish our objective.

The last few months of my tour in Afghanistan would be fast and furious and full of adventure. I never went back into the booth with that prisoner.

Timmy and I began interviewing another prisoner shortly after O'Hara left. The prisoner was supposed to be a fairly significant prisoner but we didn't realize why until we got into the booth with him. I had read the dossier on the prisoner and he was considered to be the head of Al Qaeda for all of Southeast Asia. Reading his file I pictured a large foreboding man that I would be intimidated just by being in his presence. Even looking at his picture didn't dissuade me from my mental image. When we walked into the booth the first time, I was extremely disappointed. The man was small and fragile looking just like his picture accurately portrayed. I had built an image in my head based on the guy's title and not the dossier's facts. I learned a great lesson that day. Not all prisoners are what they seem and preconceived notions can be dangerous.

We interviewed the prisoner a few times over the next couple weeks and didn't get any real information out of him other than that he admitted being who he said he was and admitted being in charge of what the dossier said he was in charge of. Seemed pretty straightforward to me. Timmy wrote up a report on the information we had gathered and we recommended he be transferred to Guantánamo. I thought that was the end of it. Case closed, as far as we were concerned.

In July of 2005, well after I had returned home from my tour of duty in Afghanistan, I read a news report about a group of prisoners that had escaped from Bagram prison in Afghanistan. The military had reported that a small band of prisoners led by Omar Al Farouq had escaped the prison. I was baffled. I lived ten feet from the prison and I spent countless days inside the walls of the prison. How could anyone escape? The conspiracy theories were forming on the internet. *He was a CIA plant. He was allowed to escape. He was implanted with a tracking device. He would lead the US to bin Laden.*

Bagram Escapees?

Not Breaking News: al Qaeda big shot and international terror operative Omar Al-Faruq (al-Farouk, al-Farouq, al-Farook, al-Faruk, Aw-Fook and sometimes Mahmoud bin Ahmad Assegaf) escaped from US custody in Afghanistan last July and has been at large and making threats ever since. This nasty cat has been turned. Al-Faruq has most certainly been recruited by the US to penetrate al Qaeda and betray the top echelon of global Islamic terrorism. Why he turned is unimportant. The real question is: why was his cover here in the West so casually yanked? Why now? I smell a double-cross.

Update: Outside the Beltway's James Joyner smells something fishy as well, saying, "This looks very, very bad on a whole number of levels. Either the U.S. military is unable to guard top al Qaeda lieutenants (although, granted, there seem to have been hundreds of them) or it is willing to allow them to escape to avoid testifying against accused abusers." So it is a cover up of something. Joyner has more blame: "not only do we let this clown escape but we don't let our ally, who turned him over to us in the first place, know about it so that they can prepare for his return and/or help recapture him? Amazing." We are not amazed.

UnSaid Theory: UnSaid thinks Omar didn't escape, but was tagged and released. "Might not be a bad idea to let him get away and have a tracker stick on him", UnSaid suggests. Like a chip implanted in his body? RFID tags? The old feeder thinks the odds that Omar is dead are getting better with every day that passes without an Omar sighting or verifiable new video. Update: Guerrilla News Network also considers that al-Faruq is working for the CIA.

Update: Yet another mess of speculation, (e.g.: "According to one fugitive Taliban commander interviewed by a NEWSWEEK reporter last week, the four men were actually exchanged in secret for captured U.S. special-operations troops."*) sprinkled with a few details , is found in Newsweek, via MSNBC.*[12]

I knew none of that speculative nonsense was true. I was confident that he would turn up again on the battlefield and probably in Iraq since he was part Iraqi and that is where most Al Qaeda were headed to kill Americans. I was right.

On September 25, 2006, Al-Faruq was killed by British troops operating in the Iraqi city of Basra[13].

I don't know if any of the conspiracy theorists and so-called insiders ever came out from under their rocks long enough to admit the astounding level of their wrongness, but I doubt it.

Special Agent Tommy and I went into the booth following a mission that captured a Taliban commander named Toran Amanullah. He was an extremely well known and highly respected Taliban commander and earned his reputation fighting against the Soviets in the 80's. He was a career military officer and had trained his entire life to be a soldier. He went to a military school as a boy and later attended the Military Academy in Kabul. From the minute we stepped into the booth with him it was apparent that he had a formal military background. The way he sat, upright and stoic, not slouched down like the Al Qaeda detainees. He was a proud man.

The first trip into the booth with him was spent getting to know him. We didn't gather a lot of relevant intelligence from him other than getting some background on other Taliban commanders and potential targets. We talked with him about his upbringing and education. The schools he attended and his long extensive history in the Afghan military.

On our second trip we changed our strategy. We knew that he had been associated with a number of other senior Taliban commanders and we focused our questioning around that. It did not take long to gain his trust and it also didn't take long for him to open up to us. The conversation didn't last a long time but then it didn't need to. We learned what we needed to learn very quickly.

A month or so later, he would be moved out of solitary into a general population cell and that would wreak havoc on the prison. As the other prisoners recognized him they began to bow down and show their respect for him. It was obvious that the majority of them knew exactly who he was and why he was there. He was quickly moved back into solitary and isolated from the rest of the prisoners. Had he been allowed to stay in the general population, he could have very quickly organized the prisoners into a riot.

Chapter 13
Navy SEALs and Squirters

I had been in Afghanistan for only a few days when a couple of heavily bearded men strode into the office looking for assistance with some captured high value targets. Our instincts were to jump up and say, "Hell yeah" but without the blessings of our task force commander it was hard to commit to helping them out. That would change after the commander's visit. Turns out they had been in Afghanistan a number of times previously and had watched as prisoners were released due to inadequate evidence. They didn't want that to happen to their most recent captives.

Louis and Brian, as I later learned they were named, were veteran U.S. Navy SEALs. I'd met SEALs before and was honored to sit next to one on a plane out of Ft. Bragg. I asked him if Navy Hell Week was as bad as it sounded.

He replied, "Imagine the worst thing you've ever been through and multiply by ten."

At that moment I was thankful I joined the Army.

These guys belonged to SEAL Team Two out of Little Creek, VA.

SEAL Team TWO, is based at Little Creek, VA. Commanded by a Navy Commander (O-5), it has eight operational platoons and a headquarters element. SEAL Team TWO's geographic area of concentration is Europe. SEAL Team TWO deploys platoons to Naval Special Warfare Unit TWO in Germany, aboard Amphibious Ships deployed to Second and Sixth Fleets, and conducts deployment for training, (DFTs) throughout the

European theater. SEAL Team TWO is the only SEAL team with an arctic warfare capability.[14]

Louis had been in the Navy for twenty-four years and had been a SEAL for a long time. He had many stories to tell, most of which I can't repeat under threat of serious bodily injury. My favorite story was about the Kennedy sisters that he met in St. Thomas in the U.S. Virgin Islands while on shore leave. But that's as far as I can go, which is too bad. You'd enjoy it, but I enjoy having all my limbs intact, so discretion will have to prevail.

Brian also was a veteran SEAL and I regret not having had more time to get to know Brian. Sadly, Brian was killed by a roadside bomb placed by Mohammed Easa and ordered by Roze Khan on May 29, 2004. Also killed in that attack was Sergeant First Class Robert Mogenson, Captain Daniel Eggers and Private First Class Joseph Jeffries. Captain Eggers and Sergeant Mogenson were both Green Berets and Private Jeffries was a PSYOP Specialist.

I wasn't on that mission, but I distinctly remember calling home and telling my wife, Karen, that Brian had been killed. Her immediate response to me was, "What are you *doing* over there?"

I just said, "I'm fine, don't worry about me."

I can't believe I actually said that after just telling her about those men dying, but I didn't know how else to respond. There's not a lot you can say that makes sense. During that call Karen was at our friends' house having dinner with them. She was upstairs with Heidi, while Heidi's husband, Jim, was downstairs reading an email with a bunch of pictures of a vehicle with the windows blown out that I had been riding in. I can't express the gratitude that I feel for Jim and Heidi taking care of Karen while I was gone. Jim was also deployed to Bosnia in 1996 and knew full well the hardship separation causes within a family. He and Heidi made the extra effort to connect with Karen even when she was very depressed and had no desire to talk with people. It was hard being gone and hard knowing that she was home alone. It eased the pressure some to know that she had friends to lean on and who cared.

The hardest part was realizing that I was actually in a war zone and people were dying. Up until Brian's death, it hadn't hit me that what we were doing was dangerous. I was flying on auto-pilot with blinders on and oblivious to the dangers around me every time I went outside the wire, which happened to be just about every day. Death could literally be looming around every curve in the road or hiding behind every village wall.

Roze Khan publicly took credit for the death of the four soldiers. From that moment on he was mentioned in every intelligence briefing that I sat through for the rest of my tour. He had made a name for himself and the American intelligence community had put him on our radar screen with a red dot. The chief of the intelligence analysis cell in Bagram made it her personal mission to track him day and night. He was like a nightmare for her and through the course of my tour the stress on her became more apparent as each day went by. I felt her pain, we all felt her pain, but nobody as much as Louis who lost his fellow Navy SEAL and best friend to Roze Khan. Louis and Brian were the first SEALs I met when I arrived and now there was only Louis.

Mohammed Easa was the mid level Taliban commander who was in charge of the ambush that took Brian's life. Once the IED was detonated, the small group of Taliban hit the convoy of SEALs and Special Forces with small arms fire. The attack didn't last long and the Taliban faded away into the hills very quickly. Mohammed Easa was later killed by Coalition forces the week of June 27 in 2005.

Mullah Dadullah is one of two key Taliban commanders still at large after fleeing last week's fighting. He telephoned Reuters yesterday and claimed that no more than eight Taliban fighters have been killed in the past week, including a Taliban commander named Mullah Mohammad Easa[15].

His death was announced by Mullah Dadullah, who also was later killed by coalition forces on May 13, 2007.

Mullah Dadullah, the Taliban's chief military commander, has been killed in southern Afghanistan according to government officials. James Bays, Al Jazeera's correspondent, was shown a body the authorities said was Dadullah's on Sunday morning. The body was shown to media in the governor's compound in Kandahar. A sheet was removed from the body up to the knee to show that part of one of the legs was missing. Dadullah lost a leg fighting Soviet forces in the 1980s.[16]

The irony of being an intelligence officer and working with a SEAL team was that most of them had no idea who I was and to this day I would estimate less than five of them would recognize me. Only a couple of them even knew my name. My job was never to make friends with these guys, it was to provide them intelligence so they could operate and fulfill their mission. My job was always to blend in and not get noticed. I would never put myself into the same category of war fighter as these guys. These guys were *"operators"* I was just an intel puke. Even as we went after high value targets, most of the SEAL team had no idea I was even on the missions. I was merely an enabler or a force multiplier. I added value but not as a shooter or a door kicker. My value came after they did the hard work and it was the hard follow-up work that drove their next mission. In an operational environment that is working efficiently, the operations will produce intelligence and that intelligence will drive more operations. It's a wonderful cycle when it works.

Our role as enablers while the assault force was hitting a compound was to provide security on the perimeter. Our job was to shoot or capture any people who tried to escape from the compound or village. We called it "Shooting Squirters" which described anybody who squirted out of the compound. Most operations were uneventful for us because nobody was able to get past the SEAL team as they pounded through. We typically listened over the radios to what was going on during the operation and knew exactly if and when shots were fired. Once the area was secured they would call us in to do the searching, handcuffing and battlefield interrogations. While only a few of them would recognize the clean-cut corporate me of today, I was given a SEAL Team 2 coin by three different members of the team. I had apparently impressed them enough for recognition at some point. I gave away two of the coins to teammates within the Criminal Investigation Task Force but I kept one for myself. It's an honor to be recognized by some of America's most elite and hard core warriors.

Chapter 14
Driver's Tests

My first experience driving with Bug was not pleasant to say the least. As I have mentioned before, driving in Afghanistan was like somehow being stuck inside a video game. Nate had been through some pretty serious driving courses and I felt completely at ease when he was behind the wheel. I never once feared for my life as I had on that first ride with Bug. Driving is one of those skills that everyone takes for granted in the United States. Being able to drive in a combat zone requires a completely different skill set. I envy the guys that are able to drive Humvees with ease. It's not an easy task and it takes a lot of practice to hone the skill. I drove Humvees all over Bosnia and we stuck out like a sore thumb. We never blended into traffic and it was blatantly obvious when the Americans were rolling into town. In Afghanistan it was the complete opposite. We never wanted anyone to know it was us showing up. We drove Toyota vehicles because everyone else in the country drove Toyotas. The only vehicle better for blending into the landscape would have been a beat up yellow taxi. I think Alice could probably have acquired one had we asked her to.

As we worked with different groups from the military and the U.S. government it seemed like we were constantly being tested to see if we were worthy of traveling outside the wire with people. They wanted to know if they would be safe traveling with us. Would we give them away? Would we make a foolish driving mistake? Being caught in the wrong place at the wrong time could cost us our lives and endanger other members of the mission. We had to know how to react quickly to changing circumstances, and how to get out of bad situations. We didn't have the luxury of armor as the Humvees did so if we did get hit our only hope was that the vehicle would keep going long enough to get us out of the kill zone. We tinted our windows so the locals couldn't see into the vehicles. Every little thing made a difference.

In mid May we made a trip down to Kabul with Lawrence, the CIA Bagram station chief. We were heading there to attend a meeting that we both attended on a regular basis but never traveled together. This was a first for us and we needed to make a good impression. Nate and I rode in his vehicle and the trail vehicle had a team from the Special Forces camp. They included one intelligence guy and two guys who had never left the wire and wanted to go sightseeing in Afghanistan. One of them was a surgeon and a full Colonel, one step from a General, who was probably extremely skilled at his craft but had no business being outside the wire. As we passed the United States Embassy in Kabul he promptly pulled out his camera and readied himself to take a picture of the embassy as we drove past. This is a huge security violation, unbeknownst to him, and the Afghan guards rushed the vehicle. They surrounded the vehicle with AK-47's poised to fire. Lawrence slammed on the brakes, slammed our vehicle into reverse, and hauled ass back to where they were stopped. Without considering any of the possible consequences to himself, he leaped out of the vehicle and confronted the lead guard. Within seconds he had managed to defuse the situation. Nate and I had also leaped out of the vehicle and backed him up with our guns raised and ready to fire. It was at that moment that we had proven ourselves to Lawrence. He accepted us and we built an incredible working relationship from that point on.

We passed his test!

A week later we were once again headed down to Kabul for the same meeting and Lawrence was unable to attend. We hooked up with the guys from the targeting cell for Joint Task Force 76 or JTF-76. They were the team who put together the Concept of Operations for the 25th Infantry Division and made recommendations on which high value targets should be raided next. They had to determine if there was enough intelligence to warrant a raid and then verify whether or not that intelligence was credible. I can't say that I envied their job. They had to make some pretty tough decisions.

I rode with Warrant Officer Manuel Ramirez. Unlike my first hair-raising experience with Bug, this was like a drive in the park. Ramirez drove well below the speed of traffic and was very cautious. He never passed another vehicle and was content to sit behind or between trucks on the highway. And yet as safe as that might sound, I felt nervous and uneasy the entire time I was riding with him. He broke every rule of driving in a hostile environment. That would be the last trip we would pair with that team. In Afghanistan and other war zones, driving like you're on the way to the mall can have severe consequences.

He failed his test!

The following week we ended up traveling with a Defense Logistics Agency (DLA) team. We could have done the entire convoy within our task force but decided that they were headed down anyway and we may as well just use them rather than risk more guys from our team. That was an incredibly poor decision on our part. The DLA guys were worse than Ramirez. They drove like Grandma on a Sunday drive to church. They took in all the sights. They rolled windows down and hung out and at one point we even heard them whistling out the window. So much for keeping a low profile and blending into your surroundings. Needless to say, we survived but we never traveled with them again either.

They failed the test!

In early June we were asked to accompany some of the SEAL team on a mission to Kabul. They said they needed us to fill out the convoy of two vehicles and to introduce them to the Human Intelligence (HUMINT) team down in Kabul. I think they really just wanted to test us and see how we handled ourselves outside the wire. It's not like a group of SEALs couldn't survive without help from us. We weren't five minutes out of Bagram Airbase when we saw an Apache helicopter go down a mile or so out in a field off to our right. It looked to us like it landed pretty hard. We weren't sure what was up so we radioed back to the SEAL team that we were stopping and radioing in to Bagram to see if they knew there was a chopper down. We were only stopped for a few minutes before it took off again and we received word back from Bagram that the helicopter was fine.

We traveled the same road we had driven dozens of times already. I felt like I could make the trip with my eyes closed if I needed to. As we started to enter the outskirts of Kabul, we came across a German military vehicle that had gone off the road and overturned. We again stopped and pulled security on the vehicle until more German soldiers arrived. It was a tense time since we were on the main drag into the city and it was a very highly traveled stretch of road for good guys and bad guys. Numerous ambushes had taken place on the road within a half mile in either direction of the spot where we were stopped.

We obviously passed the test!!!

In late July we would make another trip with a group from the SEAL team from Bagram, this time all the way down to Kandahar. It was a testament to us that they would trust us to make a trip that far. We felt like we had proven ourselves to them and they had accepted us at that point. Their approval and acceptance was better than any trophy or medal I've ever won.

Chapter 15
Fourth of July 10K and Barbeque

We had the best assortment of meat on Bagram Airbase, and maybe in the whole theater (theater being the entire Middle East). I don't how Alice procured any of the stuff she did, but somehow she was well connected. We had decided to take advantage of our bounty and hold an enormous barbeque for the upcoming Fourth of July. Then we found that there was to be a Fourth of July *Freedom Isn't Free Fun Run.*

The course for the 10k run for all of the soldiers went all the way around the airfield. It was the same route that Tommy, Don and I ran just about every day. Tommy sometimes ran it twice a day just for fun. It sounded like a lot of fun so we talked everyone on our task force into signing up to compete.

Lawrence and Alice decided that they should run together since they both thought they would be pretty slow runners. Bill just kept saying he would never finish but he would try. Don and I ran together for most of the race, then when there was about a half mile to go he just took off and left me choking on his dust. Fine, pick on the fat kid again. Nate and Bill ran together for most of the way but finished far apart. The highlight of the run was Tommy, who took third place, finishing in thirty-seven minutes. The winner of the run was, of course, from one of the Special Operations task forces that wasn't officially there so he officially didn't exist. I'm not sure if that means that Tommy really took second place but having a 'ghost' for a winner puts an interesting spin on things. Tommy's time of thirty-seven minutes was pretty darn good and this guy kicked his butt. That should tell you how fast our Special Operations soldiers really are. The Special Operations soldiers in the U.S. military are truly the best - the strongest and the fastest in the world. We can all be proud of them, even though most of their work is done in secrecy and they rarely get any kind of acknowledgement for the awesome work they do. Whatever their motivations are, it's sure as hell not fame or fortune.

After the race was over, there were the usual booths that accompanied road races that I had run in back at home. There were Gatorade booths and t-shirts and even somebody selling pins. It was weird to be in Afghanistan and yet feel like I was back in the States running a holiday race. The big difference was the grime on my teeth. The running track was laid out around the airfield, which was actually a large open space in the desert. That meant a lot of dust was kicked up by airplanes and helicopters taking off and landing all the time. As you ran around the airfield you would run through clouds of swirling dust that would coat your teeth, becoming a thick paste as it mixed with your own saliva. By the time you had finished the full six mile loop your mouth would feel like you had been eating mud for a week. It was an incredibly uncomfortable feeling but so was being in a combat zone. Having mud on my teeth was easier, I guess, than being shot at. I still to this day have 'mud mouth' flashbacks and brush my teeth five or six times a day!

The barbeque started a couple hours after the run finished. People went back to their areas and cleaned up while we fired up the grill and started preparing food. We operated like a restaurant in many aspects. We each had our own specific duties and without every one of us completing those duties the entire barbeque would have been a disaster. That just goes to show the level of teamwork and camaraderie that our task force had built. It was a lot of fun working with these guys even on something as relatively simple as a barbeque feast.

My first 'camp restaurant' job had been baker. After the bread maker had arrived from my mom, we all sent emails home letting people know to send us boxes of bread mix. Before long we began receiving every imaginable type of bread dough mix, from plain white bread, to honey wheat, cinnamon raisin, twelve grain, tomato basil, banana, and even apple cinnamon. It was awesome. The healing, comforting smells of coffee and fresh warm bread make up for a lot in a combat zone and if you close your eyes you can picture your wife or mother in the kitchen and it creates a sense of normalcy, even if only for a moment. While we had some extremely good ribs and steak off the grill, the fresh baked bread always seemed to be the biggest hit.

My second side job of course was coffee barista. I loved making lattes for everyone who wanted one, but it took me a while to get the frothing of the milk down. I was using the Army issue milk that didn't need to be refrigerated and wasn't exactly like the fresh milk used at a real Starbucks, but who were we to complain. We had fresh hot somewhat steamed lattes.

Nate and Bill typically ran the grill. Sometimes they even got a little defensive if someone else tried to step in and run it for them. Like with most all men, there is a fierce pride factor to grilling and no man likes to be shown up or told how to do it better. I had my own opinions and I like to think grilling should be a slow cooking process to really allow the meat to tenderize and cook all the way through but in Afghanistan we didn't have that luxury. We had to cook on high heat and fast because we never knew when we would be jerked away for a mission.

Tommy, Timmy and Lucky usually handled setting up the tables and got the buns and condiments ready. We never seemed to run out of condiments and again I'm not sure how that happened. In every care package, we would get bottles of ketchup and mustard and even some jars of pickles and relish. Many of the care packages even contained peanut butter and grape, strawberry or raspberry jelly. Put that with the fresh bread and a lot of our guests didn't even care about the steaks, ribs or burgers. They had a good old fashioned PB and J sandwich. Compared to the bread in the chow hall and the nasty peanut butter that gets served by KBR (Kellogg Brown and Root, the subsidiary of Halliburton responsible for feeding the troops), having a jar of JIF was golden.

We spent hours feeding and entertaining our guests, like an unauthorized USO or officer's club. We had a dart board and we opened up our internet access to people so they didn't have to wait in line over at the community center to check email. Believe me, that made us a number of new friendships.

The mystery guy who won the race earlier that day showed up along with some other guys who weren't really there. Sort of a 'ghost force'. Since none of them officially existed I guess we didn't feed them with the food we didn't have, at least that's what Alice told me. We made some pretty solid connections with the ghosts and would run a couple of missions with them. Allegedly.

We had a pretty good working and social relationship with the Air Force Office of Special Investigations (OSI) team that was operating out of Bagram too. They also had a private compound and could hold barbeques so we frequented their dwellings quite often. The team was running missions with them when I arrived but for some reason that stopped shortly thereafter. I think O'Hara went out on one of the missions and got scared by a group of little kids. I'm not making light of that, even though it sounds funny. It wasn't uncommon when you were out in a local village to have a huge group of kids swarm you and if you weren't expecting it you could get really freaked out. You felt trapped and overwhelmed and you knew you couldn't shoot your way out if one of them was armed. Whenever we went into Kabul we actually would hire one of the kids for a couple bucks as our bodyguard. The bodyguard's job was to keep people away from us. It sounds crazy but a couple bucks to these kids was a lot of money and if it meant a suicide bomber couldn't get within ten feet of me, it was well worth it. On O'Hara's first trip outside the wire with OSI and Alice he got surrounded by a group and felt really threatened. I can see why, but complaining about it only broke the relationship with OSI and we lost out on any real time intelligence that was gathered on those missions.

The interrogators from inside the Bagram prison came over that Fourth of July as well. They were a good group and at that time there were actually two overlapping sections: the outgoing group that was there when I arrived and the new team that was replacing them. The old team was led by an Army Lieutenant Dave Jones. He liked to join us on our mud-mouth runs periodically and he was great guy. He was a graduate of West Point but didn't handle himself like the stereotypical West Point grad. Usually they come off as arrogant and condescending but he wasn't like that. That probably explains why he worked in human intelligence and wasn't an infantry officer. It takes a different mindset to be in intelligence and he fit the bill. He went out of his way to ensure that we were integrated into the intelligence that came out of the interrogations performed by his team. They held a daily meeting that I attended as often as possible. I had access to their computer systems so I could download all of the interrogators' reports and upload them into the system that we used for law enforcement interviews. It was a tedious process that I wanted to automate but never had the chance. It wouldn't have taken very long to get it automated but I was pretty busy most of the time with other missions and tasks.

Those meetings actually got pretty heated on occasion. Some of the younger interrogators were still learning how to read prisoners and what approaches were necessary to break them. The Military Police were trying to use incentives to encourage the prisoners to be more cooperative and that stepped on the toes of the interrogators. Giving a prisoner a reward for supplying information was an extremely effective way to get them to talk, like the cheeseburger scenario illustrated earlier. Having the Military Police take that tool out of the interrogator's tool belt took away one of the best methods of building rapport with a prisoner.

One of the first tricks I learned from that team was that tea was an extremely effective tool to use. There is a fine line that needs to be walked and checks and balances must be in place to verify that the information is correct and the interrogators took great measures to vet the information. In many cases they knew the answer before they entered the booth and they wanted to see if the prisoner would tell them the truth. Giving rewards for incorrect information is counterproductive and the interrogator loses credibility.

The outgoing team was experienced and many of them had been in Afghanistan before and a few had also been to Iraq. They knew how to question a detainee and what techniques to use and were very professional. The new team was an Army Reserve team and wasn't nearly that experienced. The quality of the interrogation reports dropped significantly in the first few weeks of their tour. I felt bad for them that they had been thrown into the fire and had been forced to learn on the fly. It couldn't have been easy.

One of the members of the unit introduced herself to me at the barbeque. She didn't know it until I brought it up but we had served together before. She was called up back in 1998 by her PSYOP unit to fill an open slot with another PSYOP unit for a tour in Bosnia. That happened to be the same unit I was assigned to and she served with our detachment in Sarajevo. Truly a small world. Just like everyone else that I ran into from my past, she didn't recognize me. I had no idea that merely growing a beard could provide such good cover. Something to keep in mind if I ever go on the lamb.

Chapter 16
Operation "Chargers"

The mission to find and capture Ghulam Mohammed Hotak began on a scorching July night. Our Toyota Land Cruiser was positioned in the middle of the convoy as usual, only this time we had a signal intercept device strapped to the top of the vehicle. It looked like a landmine stuck to the top of the vehicle, but it allowed us to listen to the enemy around us as we were driving. The Taliban liked to talk on handheld radios that are free for all to listen to and they know that we listen to them. They have even gone as far as taunting the guards working in the towers on the perimeter of Bagram Airbase. I had no idea, however, what we would hear in less than twelve hours.

The operation we were heading out on had actually begun weeks earlier when we had started working with the HUMINT team from Kabul. They had been working with numerous sources and this one was already shaping up to be huge. He had led us to Ghulam Mohammed Hotak. Hotak and his brother Haji Musa Hotak had been legendary mujahideen commanders fighting the Soviets in the eighties. Like many tribal fighters, they changed sides every time someone new came to power. They had pledged allegiance to the Taliban at one point and retained control of the region where they lived. They grew opium and protected their land and community and no one cared. But now they had blown up some international workers and needed to be taken down.

History repeats itself. Take Mohammed Musa Hotak and Ghulam Mohammed, the two brothers known as big warlords from Wardak, a province south of Kabul, as examples. Both of them have 1,000 armed followers, who have surrendered to Commander Abdullah of the Northern Alliance. Of course, they did not do so without reservation. As their wages, they demanded authority and a region. These two brothers are nothing more than chameleons. When the mujahideen fought against the Soviets, they became mujahideen. When the Taliban was in power, they became Taliban. Now that the Northern Alliance is in power, they have joined the Northern Alliance. "This is purely business," Abdullah said.[17]

Earlier we had traveled to Kabul with the Intelligence guys from the SEAL team to meet with the HUMINT Team from Kabul and get the Concept of the Operation, or CONOP, which outlined the scope of the operation. We learned that we had a ton of intelligence on this operation, so it looked like an excellent choice of target.

During that meeting we also gathered intelligence from the Kabul team on another major Taliban commander whom I will call Mohammed Young. Mohammed Young had been attacking American forces and was supporting the insurgency throughout Afghanistan. The SEALs made the strategic decision to hit both targets back to back.

The informant who was feeding us intelligence on Mohammed Young was a man called "Stumps". He earned that name during the brutal reign of the Taliban. He was involved in a robbery, but he was merely the getaway driver. Needless to say, the criminals didn't get away and were caught by the Taliban. As we all know, the Taliban are ruthless and didn't take stealing lightly. His punishment for being the getaway driver was to have his right hand and right foot cut off. As horrible as that might sound, the rest of the team didn't fair nearly as well as Young did. Young had been a mujahideen fighter with Stumps back in the eighties fighting the Soviets. It was this connection that Stumps thought he could leverage to save himself when he was captured. He made a plea for Young to stand up and vouch for him so that the Taliban would not punish him. Young refused. It was this action that led Stumps to contact us many years later. Stumps wanted to get his revenge and had been waiting for years to have his chance. This was his chance.

Stumps had provided us with all kinds of intelligence on Young's compound. Everything from maps with directions to and of the compound, diagrams of the buildings, and even pictures taken with a digital camera. Amazingly, we even had the exact GPS coordinates of the compound because he had taken a handheld GPS and walked to the front gate and saved us a waypoint. This was an intelligence collector's dream. It almost seemed too good to be true, and we wondered secretly if it was.

The night of the operation we headed out around 2200 hours knowing it would be a long night. Our weapons and gear had been packed and ready to go for hours. As I mentioned, our Toyota Land Cruiser rolled out in the middle of the convoy, sandwiched between Navy SEALs in front of and behind us. This was my first major operation with the SEALs. Nate and I had been on a number of smaller operations coordinating with them and assisting them with getting connected to the right intelligence teams, so they finally trusted us enough to take us along on one of the big operations.

The adrenaline was flowing that night and the level of fear and excitement that had been building for the past couple days was off the charts. It was now 'go time' and we were ready.

As we cruised down the highway, our headlights barely making a pinprick in the black Afghan night, we kept our nerves under control by talking about this and that. Nate and I had been working very hard at gaining the SEALs' trust. Louis had gone to bat for us with the SEAL Commander and justified bringing us along on the mission. We knew we had to perform and show that we had value to add to the operation. We had rehearsed what would happen once we were on target. We knew our roles and responsibilities inside and out. We were ready.

We knew the mission had the potential of getting exciting - in fact; we could possibly see some real action. Stumps had told us that Young was always home on Thursday nights because he had company over. That company happened to be other Taliban commanders and his local fighters and we expected there to be between forty and sixty fighters in the compound when we got there. The SEALs were expecting a big firefight when we arrived. It was now clear that tonight had been chosen purposefully; it was no accident that we were headed out on a Thursday. The SEALs planned to use the opportunity to kill as many Taliban as they could that night. We would be out on the perimeter as part of the security force keeping the Taliban fighters from escaping the compound. Our mission that night was to shoot 'squirters' (men trying to escape by squirting through the gaps in our perimeter). We knew that Young had dug tunnels leading out of his compound that led into the orchard. That was where we were to be positioned. We fully expected to see some guys popping up out of the ground and needing to be shot or captured. That was our part of the mission.

We bumped and bounced our way down through Kabul and headed south toward Kandahar. We traveled that way for what seemed like an eternity but was actually only an hour or two. As we headed off the main highway (which wouldn't be considered enough for a county road in the U.S.) and up into the much rougher mountain roads my anxiety level rose like a thermometer in the desert. We were off the relatively safe main road and into serious bad guy territory. Anything could happen out here. It had been raining that night which was rare. In fact, I think this was the only time I actually witnessed it rain during my entire time there. We started to drive down a road that didn't seem like much of a road to me. I think it may actually have been a dried up riverbed but in the dark I couldn't tell very well. There were definitely vehicle tracks that we were following.

At one point the convoy, and our vehicle, stopped and I asked Nate what was going on. He said that we were crossing a river, but that seemed to me like an odd reason to stop the whole convoy. Maybe, I thought, the bridge is too small and they are being cautious about its ability to bear the weight of the vehicles, or maybe they had to check it for explosives. My mind was racing at that point trying to figure out what was going on. Then we rolled up and it was our turn. As we turned the corner and I saw the river in front of us I realized how silly my thoughts had been. We were driving through the river not over the river on a bridge. This was Afghanistan. A bridge would be a huge luxury. The water was less than a foot deep so even though the water was flowing pretty fast I didn't think it would be a problem. As the vehicle ahead of us, now a ghostly shape in our headlights, started to go through the river, Nate decided he could follow right behind them. We could use their tracks through the mud and get through pretty easily. Just as that vehicle was going up the bank on the far side they bounced out of our headlights and stopped. Nate suddenly had to swerve out of their tracks to avoid hitting them and we ended up sideways, sinking slowly into the mud. I couldn't even open my door because the water was rushing by so fast. Nate immediately radioed that we were stuck and jumped out to see what he could do.

As I sat there looking out into the darkness I thought to myself, *I'm a sitting duck here.* I scanned the other side of the river for movement and had my M-4 ready for whatever was going to pop up. In the meantime, the truck that was ahead of us had backed up and hooked a chain onto our vehicle. They pulled us up the bank and we were able to proceed on the mission. Muddy, but otherwise okay.

We kept driving through river banks up further into the mountains. At one point we entered a small village and we turned off all our vehicle lights. With the aid of our night vision equipment we could see everything but they didn't even know we were passing by. We passed one small mud hut and spotted a man sitting on the front step. He was perfectly still, not moving. We couldn't tell right away what he was doing there but he had a rifle next to him which was a potential problem. Randall turned on the infrared laser beam on his rifle and pointed the beam directly at the man's forehead. The narrow beam of light allowed us to see that man was actually sleeping and had no idea that he had a squad of heavily armed men watching him.

When we entered the next village we stopped again rather abruptly. I was wondering what was going on but Nate had the radio. We were trying to remain as quiet as possible so I didn't want to ask questions. After only a few minutes Nate said we needed to get out and pull security. I got out and walked a few feet up toward the front of the vehicle and looked carefully around the corner. What I saw amazed me. The Humvee that had been three vehicles ahead of us had flipped over. The road had literally split with one side going up and the other going down. The road had quite literally turned into a high road and a low road. There's a joke in there somewhere but in light of the situation at hand nobody wanted to make it. With night vision goggles on it had been darn near impossible to tell that the road split and one side went up and the other side went down. Apparently the driver veered too far to one side and the vehicle flipped over when one set of wheels went down and the other went up.

Again I had the tense feeling that we were sitting ducks, only this time I had the added eerie feeling that we were being watched. I'm not sure how long we were actually there but it seemed like forever. Maybe it was just my paranoia feeling like someone was watching us. Somehow, I doubt it. Those tribal mountain people survive by watching and knowing everything that's going on in and near their villages. I don't think the presence of a convoy of U.S. military vehicles escaped their notice.

The SEALs hooked two more Humvees up to the one that had tipped over. One hooked the side and the other one hooked up the back. As they pulled the tipped Humvee up, they had to simultaneously pull it back to get it back off the split road. It wasn't a good scenario and there was a good chance it would fail and we would lose the vehicle, but they handled it very well. I couldn't wait to see how they handled themselves under fire. These guys are truly the best of the best and I still couldn't believe that I was with them on a mission. Less than a year ago I was sitting behind a desk typing on my computer. Not a day went by since September 11 that I didn't think about going back into the Army and helping out. I never in my wildest dreams thought that I would end up in Afghanistan working side by side with elite Navy SEALs.

Once the vehicle was right side up and we were ready to roll, the commander decided to take us on a different route. We spent the next few hours searching out different routes trying to get to the target village. We ran into dead end after dead end. We would be bouncing along on a road that seemed to be going somewhere, and it would just end. Even the AC-130 Spectre gunships providing over watch had tried to guide us through the confusing labyrinth that made up the mountain passageways of Afghanistan. It proved to be a failed attempt. We couldn't find a passage to his village. I suspect that Young knew we were coming and had blockaded all of the main routes into his village with rock piles. We knew that something was wrong because Stumps had disappeared the day before the operation and never made contact again. If I had to make a guess I would say he is probably buried in a field somewhere outside of Young's village. After many frustrating hours of trying to make our way to the village, the commander called off the mission and we headed back to base.

We drove the winding roads for so long in pitch blackness that I became completely disoriented. I finally recognized the river we'd had to cross and I hoped this time we wouldn't get stuck. As the Toyota Land Cruiser in front of us went through they did get stuck this time. I had an uneasy feeling in my stomach as we had yet to cross the river. As we sat and pulled security watch while that vehicle was being pulled out of the river I reminded Nate to put to our vehicle back into four-wheel drive. We had taken it out earlier in the night and I wanted every advantage possible to get through the river. We made it without a problem.

We spent the next couple hours on the lonely drive back to Bagram. I was so incredibly tired and yet I couldn't fall asleep. I don't think I could have if I'd wanted to. The excitement and then the letdown of the mission were both physically and mentally exhausting but my adrenaline was stilling flowing pretty good. We watched the sun come up and rode home in silence.

I didn't rest much that day because I knew we had another mission coming up that night. The mission targeting Hotak was on and we had a lot of work to do to get ready. After we had cleaned our weapons and the vehicle we had to head over to the SEAL compound for rehearsals. We had a new strategy and a new role for tonight's mission. We had to be ready.

As we did the walk through of where we were to be positioned, I had a sense that tonight would be an exciting mission. After the letdown the night before, I was actually looking forward to some action. I would get what I wished for.

We tried to catch a few hours of sleep before we left but again I found that I just couldn't sleep. I ran over to the PX and picked up some sunflower seeds because I knew we would be tired. We headed back to the SEAL compound and prepped the vehicle for moving out.

The convoy rolled out and headed down toward Kabul. The village we were hitting tonight would be south of Kabul on the way to Kandahar again. We turned off the road and drove about 15 km into the mountains to the village of Meydan Shar. As we approached we went to blackout conditions and drove with only the aid of night vision equipment. We thought we would be much smarter than we had been the night before and we brought a gigantic IR flashlight that lit up the path in front of us. It was only visible to us because we had the night vision so it was invisible to the naked eye. The downside was that I had to hold it out the window and try to keep it steady as we drove down the incredibly bumpy, pot hole filled, river bed that we were using as a road. That was no small task. Nate was having trouble with his night vision and we had to stop and then play catch up which of course made all the vehicles behind us have to catch up as well. We made a quick change and Randall, whose equipment seemed to work better, took the wheel and we made it the rest of the way to the village without incident. I wish I had paid more attention to the drive out that night because it would prove to be critical the next morning as we left the village.

We moved up into our pre-assigned position on the road. The SEALs had moved into the village to begin the assault and the secondary force (a foreign Special Forces team) had moved into position watching the rest of the perimeter. We were the enablers or force multipliers. We had no business being part of the assault team and they knew that as well as we did. We would wait on the perimeter and watch for squirters. There were always plenty of those poor bastards that tried to escape. In this case the squirters would try to leave through the area being watched by the secondary force. That would be a costly mistake for them.

As we waited for the assault to begin, the air was thick with tension and the excitement level was pegged on high. This SEAL team was already on track to capture or kill more senior Taliban than any other unit thus far in the war. This mission would no doubt add another high-value enemy commander to their credit.

After a short time spent impatiently waiting on the road and watching the static horizon for movement, we heard the unmistakable blast from the breaching charge the SEALs used on the door. We were at least a half mile away and yet we heard it loud and clear. A minute later we heard the radio call, "Shots fired, shots fired!"

It was unclear from our position where the shots had come from but the SEALs knew the exact location. They had come from the compound next door to the one they had hit. It belonged to Haji Musa Hotak, the brother of the warlord that we were after. Both of them were very obviously as dirty and as involved in terrorism as the day is long, but we were under strict marching orders *not to touch* Haji Musa due to his connections to the Karzai government. That rule gets changed instantly when the enemy decides to shoot at us. The SEALs split into two teams and assaulted both compounds at the same time.

From the road we had no idea what was happening, other than what we could glean from listening to the radio traffic. We knew that shots had been fired from within the Haji Musa Hotak compound and also from the orchard. I found out when we moved into the compound that two men had made a run to retrieve some weapons stashed out in the orchard and when they picked them up to fire the secondary team lit them up. They almost blew the arm right off one of the Taliban fighters.

Now here's a prime example of how the American and Allied troops differ from our enemies. The team moved forward and subdued the men and the medic from the secondary team *saved the man's life*. He would have been dead within an hour if he had not received medical attention. Not only did they provide aid, they called in a medi-vac unit and had the man flown back to Bagram Airbase to have his arm repaired. Unfortunately for him, since he had fired on us, he would be sent right over to the Bagram Airbase prison when his wounds healed. I can't imagine that had any of us been wounded, we would have received such compassionate treatment.

It would take almost an hour before we got the call to head into the village. That meant that the compounds were secured. The reality is that it meant the main compound had been secured and the rest of them were in progress but the SEALs needed us to do our job and manage the prisoners and searching the compounds so they could continue to move out and clear the remaining compounds.

We jumped into our vehicles and started to drive up the narrow road that led up to the compounds. It was dark and I had one of the SEALs guiding me in as I drove into the village. We went around all of the Humvees that were parked on the road and pulled into a ditch that was next to the wall of the Haji Musa Hotak Compound. I learned first hand that depth perception is gone when driving with night vision when I pulled too far forward into the ditch and hit the bank pretty soundly. The brush guard on the Land Cruiser was bent up and I thought maybe I had really messed up the vehicle. Bill would not be happy with me when we got back tomorrow. As it turned out, the brush guard was the least of the damage to the vehicle that night.

I went to the back of the vehicle and grabbed my backpack. I had an ordinary Camelback, Desert Camouflage backpack that you can buy in the Post Exchange or PX (military equivalent to Walmart) at Ft. Benning. It wasn't the cool Blackhawk backpacks that the SEALs and the Special Forces guys had but it did the job. I used it to carry my flex cuffs, fingerprint gear, cameras and a lot of Ziploc bags and Sharpie markers. All of the stuff that we used to bag and tag evidence and intelligence while on target.

As I moved into the main compound I saw that a team of SEALs had a large man in their custody, standing outside against a wall. As I watched, they slowly moved him toward the Land Cruiser that had followed us into the village. The detainee stood beside the darkly tinted window of the vehicle. I knew that this was the HVT (high value target) we were after from having studied his physical description and his picture, but the SEALs wanted absolute verification of his identity.

The passenger inside the vehicle, sitting safely behind the tinted window, was the source that had led us to him. He was no doubt identifying Ghulam Mohammed Hotak.

I walked a few steps further and passed through the opening where the compound door had been, before it had been blown off its hinges. This was obviously where the shaped charge had been used to great effect and just inside the opening was a car with all its windows blown out. He had definitely parked too close to the door on this night. The house was extremely large by Afghan standards and was painted a

bright garish blue. That was unusual and it meant Ghulam
Mohammed Hotak was a wealthy and important man. To live in a
house decorated this way meant he was prominent and doing pretty
well financially. The front porch was roughly ten feet deep and
twenty-five feet wide. I went up the steps and into the house. The
first thing I noticed was all the women and children huddled in the
room straight ahead that looked to be the kitchen. One of the female
MP's was guarding them. Most of them seemed to be crying or
sobbing but I couldn't see any faces because they all were wearing full
burkas. Only their eyes were visible. The MP seemed to have them
well under control so I moved on.

Past the staircase was where all the commotion was going on. I
went back toward the noise at the rear of the house, and entered a
room where all the men considered to be of fighting age had been
herded. They were all seated on the floor facing the wall and had been
restrained with flex cuffs. Nate ordered me to stand guard on this
room for a few minutes so I immediately reached for my flashlight. It
wasn't there. All I had was my tiny little LED flashlight with a red
bulb. I felt like an ass for not having my flashlight but at that point
there wasn't much I could do. I kept my rifle moving and paced up
and down the room making sure that each and every prisoner knew
that I was watching them. If they uttered a word I immediately shut
them up. The last thing I wanted was for the prisoners to being talking
to each other and coming up with a plan to escape.

FBI agent Frank Minetti was with us on the mission. He had the
laptop computer with the database of terrorists and bad guys that we
would systematically log each and every one of these guys into.
Throughout the night we took pictures of each man found in the
compound and subsequently each man that was found in the Haji

Musa Compound. They were later brought over and placed in the front room of the house away from the ones I was now guarding.

While I was in the back room, Nate, Louis and Frank popped in and out of the room checking on me and the prisoners. At one point I heard them questioning Ghulam Mohammed Hotak in the next room. They were asking if he had seen another HVT whom we were told at the last minute would be having dinner and spending the night here. I'll call him Andrew Danger. Andrew was a senior level Taliban commander who most likely took his marching orders directly from the Supreme Taliban commander, Mullah Mohammed Omar. It was believed that Hotak was working for Andrew. When Ghulam Mohammed Hotak began denying that he knew Andrew Danger, the person questioning him immediately used the "all knowing" angle that we had information already and knew he was lying. We used the name of another Taliban commander named Toran Amanullah to justify this information. Amanullah and Hotak were bitter rivals and since Amanullah had been captured and Hotak knew it we could say that Amanullah had dimed him out. Hotak continued to adamantly deny that he knew anyone named 'Andrew Danger'.

Frank entered the room and began to thoroughly search it. He asked one of the younger men about a pistol that was supposedly stashed in the room. Of course, everyone in the room denied knowing about any such pistol. Frank tore apart the bookshelf and actually pulled it completely out from the wall. This was a pretty common way for the Afghanis to hide weapons. They had entire caches of weapons hidden behind bookshelves, in window sills and under rock piles. They very inventively hid stuff everywhere and therefore we had to look everywhere. Frank found a pistol stashed inside the bookshelf. That spooked me a little since I had been in the room guarding these guys for well over an hour and there had been a pistol lurking within reach the entire time. I assumed that the rooms had been cleared. In this case it obviously had not been cleared.

It was about this time, while I was still shaken about the hidden weapon, that I encountered Norbert, our interpreter, for the first time that night. He was also visibly shaken and I didn't know why. I found out later that Norbert had been brought in shortly after the assault team's entry and had witnessed the subduing of Ghulam Mohammed Hotak. The SEALs used their standard procedure and marked him with a Sharpie. They slashed a big "NC" on his back, indicating to everyone on the team that this man was considered non-compliant. That meant he had fought back when they captured him and probably also meant that he got smacked a few times before he stopped fighting. He also had been going for the AK-47 next to the bed and is probably very lucky he didn't get to it in time or he would be dead and not just bruised and branded NC. For us he was more valuable alive and we needed to keep him that way. We stacked up his personal AK with the rest of the weapons we'd found in the house out on the porch to be logged as evidence later on.

As Nate and Louis were questioning Hotak, he apparently had become unruly again. He tried to get up and Nate used standard law enforcement tactics to convince him to stop struggling. Norbert, the interpreter, apparently did not like the tactics and began complaining, saying that we had captured the wrong guy.

I was eventually relieved of guarding the prisoners by one of the SEALs and went outside with Tommy to perform another task. We went to the back yard and began to search the space under the house. We found a treasure trove of detonators and other dangerous looking items and called over a Navy EOD Tech, to have him take a look at what we had found. An Explosive Ordinance Division Technician or EOD Tech is the bomb expert for the team. He told us they looked like the detonators that the CIA had handed out back in the eighties to fight the Soviets. There was no real good way to confirm where they got the detonators but it didn't really matter. Hotak had detonators that could be used to make roadside bombs. This was just one piece of the puzzle and we had to find the rest of the evidence.

The space under the house was also being used for storage of wood and hay. As I searched down there the only thing I could think: What a great place for a cobra to be hiding. We moved and pawed through a ton of junk down there but never found anything substantial. Just like the bookcase, though, this is exactly the type of place they like to hide weapons. You could pull a perfectly ordinary looking rock out of the wall and find a couple of hidden rifles or even an RPG. Sometimes it might only be a pistol.

The people of Afghanistan have been fighting wars for almost three decades straight, with a long history of conflict even before that, and they are good at knowing how to hide weapons from us. They have spent a lot of time and put a lot of thought into preparing their homes for war. Many homes had escape tunnels dug beneath them so that they could easily scoot out into an orchard at the first hint of trouble. The bookcase was a prime example of a hiding space. This time it was small and only concealed a small space suitable for hiding a pistol, but many times we have found similar bookcases concealing the entrance to an entire secret room where people will hide out until the area is all clear. I can't say I blame them, because during the Taliban's reign of terror they might very well get yanked out of their home and shot for not complying with the new laws.

The courtyard was filled with huge piles of junk as well. There was an outhouse in the back corner with a cart next to it that I can only presume was used to haul hay and manure. The car with the windows blown out was still sitting untouched by the entrance. There were a couple of trees in the opposite corner of the property from the outhouse. We decided we better search the grounds for a trapdoor that may be the exit for an escape tunnel. If it were going to come out any where, this would be the ideal spot. There was a small door hidden behind the tree that they could possibly sneak out when they came up out of the hole. We didn't find one but that doesn't mean it absolutely wasn't there.

I moved around to the front of the house and found Nate completing an inventory of the items that we had pulled from inside the house. I called over an interpreter and we went through the names in the cell phone. When I saw one of the names in the phone my jaw dropped and my heart pounded. I wanted to yell it out, but of course didn't dare. You would recognize the name immediately if I were able to reveal it here, but unfortunately that is forbidden. Just trust me, it was a big name. There were multiple phones pulled off the prisoners but most of them didn't have any good information. The phone with that particular HVT name was the phone that belonged to Hotak. That was a big clue that no matter what he might say to the contrary, he was still very well connected to the Taliban. On the front porch of the house there were a variety of weapons on display including a number of AK 47's, an RPG or two and a number of pistols. The Russian made AK-47's were all decorated. They had been wrapped in colorful tape and glitter. It was like nothing I had ever seen before. The SEALs and Green Berets I worked with all made sure their weapons were camouflaged and couldn't be seen. These guys seemed like they wanted the weapons to be seen. Hotak had a pretty cool leather hand-tooled pistol belt that reminded me of something you would see on a gunslinger in an old western movie. After we had finished inventorying all of the weapons and gear I moved back into the house and found myself guarding the prisoners again.

It was early morning by now and the sun had come up. I've been a lot of places, but I can't say that the sunrises in Afghanistan were anything spectacular. You were just usually glad to see the sun come up because it meant you had survived another day.

The group of prisoners I was guarding now was in the front room of the house and I didn't recognize any of them. Then I realized that these men must have been brought over from the compound next door that belonged to Haji Musa Hotak. At about the same moment that I came to that conclusion, Louis walked into the room and pointed at a large man in white clothing and let me know he'd be talking to him very soon and to be sure to keep a close eye on him. That man, I figured, was Haji Musa Hotak. He just sat there quietly and glared daggers at us, his expression screamed hatred.

Louis was moving in and out of the room bringing one prisoner back and selecting a new one to talk to. One of the younger prisoners located towards the back of the room was whining and rocking back and forth. He looked up at me and began to plead for something in Pashto. I warned him to shut up, telling him in a voice so harsh that he couldn't mistake the message. It's amazing how your voice, your language, and your demeanor deteriorate when you get into a situation like this. Nate had definitely put on his game face as had Louis, and we were all very different people now. We meant business and we wanted these detainees to know it. We wanted to make sure they took us seriously, because if they didn't we knew they would try something and put everyone - themselves and our team - in jeopardy. War does that to people - you have to adapt and change to survive and to win - and that's a side of me that I never want my wife or my daughter to see.

A young Afghani man being held in the room looked up at me, pointed to another detainee and said in clear, nearly perfect English, "He wants to go to the bathroom."

I asked him where he had learned to speak English so well and he replied, "At university."

He was obviously a very intelligent young man so I proceeded to have a conversation with him about who he was and why he was there. He identified most of the people in the room for me, at least the ones he knew. Many of them were out of town guests that were staying with the family. One of the men was obviously Arabic and not Afghani. After a while seeing so many faces it becomes pretty easy to identify the ethnic background from the facial features and even the growth patterns of the beards.

As I continued my casual conversation with the young man, many jumbled thoughts began bouncing around in my head. I had near instant rapport with him and he was readily answering any question that I asked him. I started to probe a little more and asked about weapons caches. He admitted that they had a couple big caches very close by. At that point Louis brought back another prisoner and I suggested that Louis take this guy out next and ask him about the weapons caches. The guy was a gold mine of information and we quickly relayed the information out to SEALs searching the nearby compounds. Sure enough, within minutes they found a huge weapons cache that we surely would have missed.

Even though it was beginning to become light outside, I still didn't know what time it was or how long we had been on target. Between the many tasks, interrogating prisoners, and the sheer tension we had been experiencing, I was becoming very tired. At one point as I continued to watch the prisoners, I felt my eyes closing. It was as though I had no control over them, like they were weighted with lead.

As I realized what was happening to me, I suddenly became hyper alert and aware of my surroundings. I thought to myself, *I am falling asleep at my post. I've been trusted to watch these prisoners and I am failing.* Then it hit me! That is exactly what happened to Michael Spann. He didn't fall asleep but had found himself alone and surrounded by a bunch of prisoners. In that instant the prisoners took advantage of him, rushed him and he lost his life. I wasn't about to let these guys take me. I remembered that I had brought something for just this moment.

I walked out of the room, onto the front porch and opened my backpack. Inside I had brought a gigantic bag of sunflower seeds. I took a huge handful and put them in my mouth. Sunflower seeds were my saving grace many times while driving in college. I always used them on road trips to keep me awake and alert. In this case I believe they saved my life. I hadn't realized how tired I was after the mission last night and now this mission stringing on for untold hours. I was so tired and so intent on my other duties that I had been oblivious to what was going on out in the compound.

An estimated seven hundred villagers had shown up to protest. The SEALs had been out talking with some of the village elders and they were threatening to riot if we did not release the Hotak brothers. The SEALs wouldn't have it. They began to throw flash bang grenades to back the crowds up. The villagers began to build stone walls to prevent us from driving out.

I continued to work with the prisoners while all this was taking place outside. Tommy showed up and we worked in tandem for about forty-five minutes taking the prisoners to use the bathroom. We were the softies I guess, and had compassion. The SEALs said let them piss themselves.

Suddenly Nate rushed in and said, "Get your gear, we gotta go and now!"

I didn't know what the rush was but I suspected something was up. I sure wasn't gonna argue. Leaving was fine by me. Louis and I had a quick discussion about whether or not to cut loose all the flex cuffs. Wisely we decided not to. Louis and I went into the room that housed all of the prisoners taken in Ghulam Mohammed Hotak's house and told them to wait until they heard a big boom and then they could go. It was actually quite funny watching him describe a 'big boom' to a bunch of prisoners who didn't speak English. As we walked out of the house with our gear, we joked about the look on the prisoners' faces as the concept of a 'big boom' became clear.

I walked over to our vehicle and found that it had been moved and placed in line with the rest of the convoy for our departure. I took a much needed piss against the wall of Haji Musa Hotak's compound, letting a lot of the tension of the night flow from my body. It occurred to me then that I hadn't gone to the bathroom in more than twelve hours. Maybe subconsciously I was marking the spot, like an animal. 'I was here.' In reality, I had been so involved with the handling of prisoners that I hadn't realized I had to go, even with all of the prisoners asking me to let them go.

As I climbed into the back of the Land Cruiser Nate said, "Roll the windows down, 'cause it's not over."

I wondered what the hell he meant by saying it wasn't over. *All we gotta do is drive home now, right?* I thought. Man, was I ever wrong.

Tommy climbed in and rode shotgun. Randall sat directly behind Nate and our interpreter sat behind Tommy. The interpreter began listening to the radio traffic and told us he was hearing a lot of chatter about setting up an ambush to attack the Americans as they were leaving. As he relayed this developing plot to the team in the vehicle, there was utter stunned silence. These people never quit. We relayed the ambush plot to the SEALs but it really didn't matter too much. We had to drive through it to get out of the village and we didn't have a choice. We would have to fight our way out of the village.

Then the convoy began to move. The first thing I noticed was the sound of the .50 caliber machine gun that I knew was mounted on the lead Humvee. The deep thumping sound that weapon made as the rounds were fired was unmistakable. Then I heard the easily identifiable sound of an AK returning fire but I couldn't tell where it was coming from. As we rolled down the road we had come in on, I could now see what I couldn't the night before. We had traveled over a very narrow road, not much more than a pathway, and we were back on it now. On one side of the road stood the wall of a compound and on the other side there was a dry river bed with a short wall preventing us from going off the road on that side. When we moved beyond the end of the compound wall the area opened up to a large flat field that was now filled with hundreds of angry screaming villagers. This was clearly a mob of extremely pissed off people!

What I didn't know, and only later found out, was that the SEALs had received direct orders from General Barno, the head of all coalition forces in Afghanistan, to release Haji Musa Hotak immediately. The release had actually been taking place while I relieved myself against the wall of the compound. There's a message in there somewhere.

As we rolled out I wondered what the hell would happen next. I thought about my wife back home and I knew she would be upset to hear about this mission. I wasn't even into the kill zone yet and I was already wondering how my wife would react. Not good. I needed to get through the kill zone first and not be distracted by outside thoughts. Once again, I put home and family out of my mind and concentrated on what was going on around us.

We moved maybe a quarter of a mile before coming to a complete stop. The time we sat stopped ticked by, second by second, and felt like an eternity. We were all wired from not sleeping, jacked up on adrenaline, armed and ready for a fight, and yet being held back like race horses behind the gate. The halt lasted only about thirty seconds but we all kept asking each other "what the fuck is going on?"

I could see the mob of people in the field next to the road and I could hear gunfire all around us. Should we be shooting back? At who? We didn't seem to be taking any direct fire at this point, but we felt like stationary targets. Like sitting ducks. I was completely confused by what was happening and I think everyone else in the vehicle was too. Nate just kept saying things like "keep your eyes open" and "watch these asshole's in the field".

I had the rear of the vehicle covered and I watched intently as we slowly crept further down the road. Somebody, I don't know who, said this was beginning to feel like Bakara Market. Bakara Market was the infamous scene of the tragedy for the US Army Rangers in Somalia. Those soldiers had to fight their way out of swarming crowds and it was impossible for them to tell who was shooting and who wasn't. To me, the entire mob I was looking at standing out in the field was armed. I could see people with AK's and they seemed to be the only people I saw. It might have been a trick of perception, but I saw no unarmed people.

Just as we started moving, barely inching forward, the passenger side window next to Randall shattered. I couldn't tell if it was a bullet or a rock that had been thrown. I took my eyes off of my zone of defense, the rear of the vehicle, for a few seconds as I turned and looked up to see Randall firing out the broken window. He was screaming a litany of profanity out the broken window at the people in the field. I swiveled my head back to check out what was happening behind the vehicle, and Nate chose that moment to ask if anyone had been hit.

Again, I turned my head back toward the front of the vehicle to answer Nate's question, and in that instant the back window exploded. Nate asking that question, and me turning my head to answer him, is what I believe saved my eyes. Had I been facing my window my face and eyes would have been shredded by the exploding glass. Now the vehicle had two shattered windows, mine and Randall's. The left side of my face was peppered with small shards of glass, and my beard was also full of glass. I immediately began firing out the broken window, spraying the field with gunfire. I couldn't tell where my first few shots ended up and I didn't see anyone in the field go down. It would have been nearly impossible not to have hit something or someone but I am truly not sure if I connected with any targets.

What I remember most about those few moments was the deafening sound of the weapon firing from inside the vehicle. The sound reverberated through the SUV, which was still semi-enclosed and not very large. Sort of like a fire cracker in an elevator. It will deafen you. To make matters worse, I had taken my earplugs out hours before and hadn't thought it was necessary to put them back in just for what we thought would be an uneventful drive home.

I kicked out the rest of the remaining glass in the rear window and began firing downward toward the feet of the people that were trying to rush the vehicles. I used my rifle barrel to sweep the edges of the windows and knock the glass down as close to the frame as possible. This opened up my range of fire and allowed me a wider field of vision. It also exposed more of me to the enemy. Before the window was broken I had been somewhat hidden by a very darkly tinted window. Now I was sitting there in plain sight for the raging villagers to see. We still weren't moving very fast and I was anxious to get the hell out of the kill zone. It felt to us like the convoy was stalled and couldn't move forward, but it wasn't until much later that I found out why. The industrious villagers had been busy during the night building stone walls across the roads to keep us from getting out. When you think about these people in the context of modern warfare, it's kind of amazing what they can do with nothing but rocks.

The lead Humvee had been forced to smash through the walls and was trying to make a pathway for the rest of the convoy. As I looked out the back window to see how the convoy behind us was doing I noticed that the other Toyota Land Cruiser in the convoy had sustained a blown tire. The driver side front tire was completely flat and the driver, one of the handlers of the informant, seemed to be having a lot of trouble keeping it on the road, but so far he was managing. I yelled up to Nate to radio in and let the convoy know that the vehicle had a flat. There wasn't much we could do at that point. Stopping to change the tire meant staying longer in the kill zone. Driving on it meant possibly going into the ditch or crashing but as long as they could keep it moving and on the road that was what mattered. We all wanted to get out of the situation we were in and the tire could be changed in a safer place.

The swarming villagers seemed never ending. The sea of people just kept coming and kept coming, and what had seemed like a short drive in the night before now seemed an endless road out. It had seemed like such a quick drive with the SEAL guiding me in with night vision goggles just the night before. Other than the broken windows and the blown tire, it didn't seem as though we had sustained much real damage and the level of gunfire had dropped dramatically once we began firing back. To keep it that way, we fired periodic rounds into the ground to back the crowd away. Then we waited anxiously for the next attack to come. We could clearly see men with rifles and RPG's waiting in the crowd and watching us from the rooftops. As quickly as the shooting had started, however, it had stopped. Silence, dead silence. That spooked me more than the gunfight.

We finally pulled out of the village and onto the road, if you could call it that, leading back to the main road toward Kabul. The entire incident lasted for mere minutes but when you are under attack it seems like a lifetime. We drove a few kilometers up the road and pulled a hasty security perimeter, spreading out alongside the road and making sure no bad guys were able to sneak up on us. If anyone had come forward they wouldn't have lasted long. We were as nervous and hair-trigger jumpy as we had ever been.

The guys in the Toyota behind us radioed that they didn't have a jack for their vehicle. That was unbelievable to me. My team's diligence and attention to detail meant that we checked for critical equipment every time we left base. A jack was a critical piece of equipment to us. They also didn't have a spare tire. As soon as we stopped I jumped out and pulled our jack and spare tire out for them to use. When I rolled it back to the vehicle, however, I quickly realized that our tire was too big. Fortunately for them, it turned out that there was a third Toyota Land Cruiser in the convoy that day. I hadn't even noticed it when we left late the night before, because it was behind us in the convoy. Luckily for the guys behind us, the tires were a match. We were able to get the tire changed very quickly and got the convoy moving again. The rest of the trip back to Bagram Airbase was uneventful, but we were grateful for some time to allow our adrenaline levels to subside and our hearing to return. The wind coming in through the blown out windows was a constant reminder of how close we had come to serious injury or death. As it was, all I had sustained were some nicks and cuts on one side of my face from the flying glass.

When we arrived back at base and were greeted by Bill and Chief, they were pale with worry. They had been listening to the message traffic coming in about the mission and heard that we had been ambushed by nearly a thousand Afghanis. I hadn't thought about it too much until the point when they told me that. A thousand villagers? Damn, there were only about sixty SEALs and a couple of Land Cruisers with coalition force troops tagging along. We might have been slaughtered had the villagers really wanted to hit us hard. We had seen the weapons they had, and their numbers were staggering. Where had that many people even come from? The village was small. I also couldn't figure out what had saved us. Why hadn't the big attack we were expecting happened?

We checked the prisoners into the temporary holding facility at Bagram Airbase prison, in accordance with regulations. Ghulam Mohammed Hotak was now a captured man and in U.S. custody. We had gathered and documented enough evidence to keep him in jail for a long time and more than likely get him transferred to Guantánamo. Our mission was accomplished, or so we thought. We were proud of our work and glad we had survived the mob that had tried to over-run us.

Our interpreter, Norbert, disappeared the next day and no one saw him for about a week. Nobody on the task force knew where he had gone and we were all concerned about him. That is until he returned and we figured out what he had done. Norbert had gone to Kabul to protest the arrest of Hotak and proclaimed that we had captured the wrong man. Not only was he the wrong man, Norbert now said, he accused Nate and the SEALs of abusing Hotak when he was captured. I won't deny that Hotak was probably smacked around some during his capture, because I am just as sure that he resisted arrest. I wasn't there of course, but I guarantee that anyone who resists in any way when a team of SEALs enters his home in the middle of the night is bound to get smacked. He could have chosen to surrender peacefully, so that was his own fault. The second incident occurred later when he tried to get up and Nate subdued him with what are standard law enforcement techniques. I'm not talking Rodney King style beatings here. Nate used standard grasping techniques employed to control a prisoner. Once Nate had him on the ground he applied pressure to Hotak to make sure he couldn't get up. In a war zone the last thing you want is for the prisoners to get the upper hand. They have to be controlled at all times. That's exactly what took place. The prisoner was controlled, not abused.

The coalition authorities in Kabul opened an investigation and interviewed everyone who had been present. They took sworn statements from a number of SEALs and Nate. They even interviewed the prisoner who loudly proclaimed that he had been severely abused and should therefore be released immediately. Big surprise there. What did they expect him to say? Of course he had no visible injuries to back up his claim of abuse.

The second major consequence of capturing Hotak was the uproar it caused within the Karzai government. Karzai and Haji Musa Hotak were very well connected and Haji Musa had even tried to gain a governorship and a seat in parliament. Haji Musa traveled to Kabul and petitioned the Karzai government to get his brother released. Karzai called the US military commanders and demanded that Hotak be released. We had to prepare our evidence very quickly if we were going to keep him in jail. This was turning into a huge political battle. Quite often there is conflict and disagreement between U.S., coalition, and Afghan government interests, and who should be considered a 'bad guy'. It is a dance on the head of a pin and too often the troops are the ones that get pricked.

Two nights after the mission's conclusion we had created an elaborate PowerPoint presentation documenting the entire bucket-load of evidence that we had collected against Ghulam Mohammed Hotak. He should not and would not be released because we had methodically and painstakingly documented each and every piece of evidence. That was our mission in Afghanistan. To ensure that when senior Taliban and Al Qaeda are captured that the evidence is documented so they don't get released. We had done that in this case and it was extremely gratifying to know that we had done the right thing. We had done our job well.

Here's how the western media reported what had happened:

Ex-Taliban Commander Seized in Afghanistan
July 19, 2004

KABUL, Afghanistan - U.S. forces have detained a former Taliban commander near the Afghan capital, two months after feting him for backing the country's new order, officials said Sunday.

American troops seized Ghulam Mohammed Hotak in Wardak province, southwest of Kabul, on Saturday, according to Defense Ministry spokesman Gen. Zaher Mohammed Azimi. Mohammed, his brother, and one of his nephews were detained "because they have links to the Taliban," Azimi said.

Azimi didn't elaborate, and U.S. military officials could not immediately be reached for comment. Police chief Basir

Salangi said American soldiers surrounded Hotak's house in a village near the provincial capital, Maydan Shahr, after dark on Saturday.

"Helicopters came in the morning and took him away," Salangi said.

Salangi said up to 700 people spent nine hours demonstrating in front of government offices in Maydan Shahr on Sunday, chanting for Hotak's release.

A powerful local leader, Hotak switched allegiance to the Taliban as they conquered much of Afghanistan in the mid-1990s and was a front-line commander against the opposing Northern Alliance.[18]

We traveled down to Kabul the next day and delivered the PowerPoint presentation to the coalition investigation team, as well as the prison board for their review. It had already been delivered to the commanding general at Bagram Airbase for his review. Now it was on the desk of General Barno, the very man who ordered us to release Hotak's brother, Haji Musa Hotak. We suddenly had sinking feelings in our stomachs. Could he release this brother too? Surely not. But it didn't happen because we were very good at our jobs. The evidence that had been compiled and properly documented stood up and everyone came to the same conclusion: Ghulam Mohammed Hotak should remain in prison.

We made a stop on that trip to visit the guys who had been in the Toyota behind us on the mission. They were just as grateful as we were to have made it out alive. They agreed that the whole situation could have been very ugly and disastrous for us all. As we talked with them we learned another valuable piece of information about what transpired that day. (That's how things work in the military. Nobody has the complete picture, each person sees a tiny part of the whole mission.) We knew these guys from the Landcruiser behind us were also the guys who had been handling the informant who had led the SEALs into the village. They met with the informant the day after the mission and the informant relayed information he found out when he returned to the village. Haji Musa Hotak, the brother that was released, had called off the ambush shortly after it began. The enemy fighters watching us leave had been ready to kill us all. I think I turned as white as school glue when I heard that. I suddenly realized the enormity of the disaster that had been averted that day. But don't be mistaken and think that the ambush was called off out of some humanitarian concern for our lives. Haji Musa Hotak's motive was purely a selfish one. He knew that his brother and his son had been taken as prisoners and were somewhere in the convoy, but he didn't know which vehicles they were in. He didn't want to risk them getting killed in the battle. He also knew the ferocity of the Navy SEALs and had great respect for their abilities to rain down hellfire on the villagers. If the ambush had continued any longer, the battle would have turned out very badly for both sides. While the losses on our side would have been unavoidable and high because we were so outnumbered, the losses to the villagers would have been much higher. The SEALs would have systematically taken them apart and hundreds of Afghani fighters and villagers would have died that day. Hotak knew that and wanted his men to survive to fight another day. He had used a cell phone and called the men on the rooftops and they relayed the message throughout the villagers not to attack the Americans. As much as I despise Haji Musa Hotak for who he is and what he has done, I admire him for his conviction that day. His decision, even if selfishly motivated, saved the lives of not only Americans but hundreds of Afghanis. He made the right choice to call off the attack.

Chapter 17
Al Farouk and Tarnak Farms

A week after the Hotak mission, we set out on one of the most critical missions in which I would participate. We started early in the pre-dawn hours and it was mid July and already very hot. Everyone assigned for the mission showed up at the airfield and we checked our gear and then checked it again. We made sure everything was in working condition and then headed over to prepare for entering through the rear-loading ramps of the massive Chinook helicopters. I had been doing this drill over and over again since I got to Afghanistan. A few times we had gone out on Black Hawks designed for carrying troops, but mostly the huge Chinooks choppered us from mission to mission.

Al Farouk had become a primary training facility for Al Qaeda in the late nineties. Dozens of senior level Al Qaeda and Taliban had been through the legendary camp and received training. A few notable names, now being held at Guantánamo Bay, are Benyam Mohammed, David Hicks, John Walker Lindh and the Lackawana Six (the six men arrested for having ties to Al Qaeda). Additionally, a number of September 11 hijackers attended training at the camp, including Saeed Ghamdi, Ahmed al-Nemi, and brothers Wail and Waleed al-Shehri. Our sensitive site exploration of this camp would eventually provide overwhelming evidence for the coming tribunals that these men trained here. Al Qaeda recruits received training in the use of small arms such as the Kalashnikov rifle, PKM automatic rifle, Makarov pistol and RPGs (Rocket Propelled Grenade launchers). There were also classes in bomb making and explosives.

A large mosque was the centerpiece of the camp compound, and this was where every Muslim recruit had attended prayer sessions. This mosque was also once a favorite place for Osama Bin Laden and Ayman Al-Zawahari to give inspirational lectures to the recruits. During one lecture in the summer of 2001, he mentions a martyr mission for twenty members. On one end of the camp was the main living area where the recruits rested and slept. The other end of the camp held the training area and shooting range. On the mountainsides surrounding the camp were defensive fighting positions meant to protect the camp from invasion.

We brought along SSG Smith from the Combined Joint Special Operations Task Force (CJSOTF) HUMINT Team. He had enabled me to make connections to so many teams, which is in large part what made us so successful. I thought that I should return the favor, so I talked with Chief about it. He readily approved bringing along SSG Smith.

The team from the Defense Intelligence Agency or DIA sent a representative named Kurt. He was a former Navy SEAL and had since moved on to work for DIA. I went to Kabul with him a few times when they needed another body and a rifle to fill out the convoy. We paired with other groups that way quite frequently. Since most intel and law enforcement teams are relatively small they always need an extra body or two for additional firepower in the vehicle. It was a common practice to help each other out.

The FBI had a team stationed south of the camp down in Kandahar. Two of those guys, Scott Gorman and Sam Diamond, would accompany us on the mission. A third FBI agent, JP Hewitt, out of Bagram Airbase, would also tag along. Hewitt was my sometime partner playing Halo on the Xbox we had in our B-hut. We were both pretty good at the game and could clear levels fairly easily.

It is amazing the things you get good at in your spare time in a combat zone. As soldiers, we are constantly transitioning, shifting gears, from heart pounding action to mind numbing boredom, and games help. At least for me they do.

The 25th Infantry Division (ID) needed to have a support group of guys tagging along as well so we requested a team of EOD experts. I would have preferred to have the SEALs' EOD guys with us, but we didn't have much of a choice.

As we waited on the tarmac we all joked about the ungodly heat for so early in the morning. We had no idea what we were in for that day and the anticipation and the uncertainty was eating away at all of us. Nobody had been to the camps since early in the war and we were told they were still empty. But you never know in Afghanistan. For all we knew bin Laden could have stopped by and used the place for shelter for a night on his rounds from hiding place to hiding place. Maybe he left us some evidence. Maybe he was even still there. It was a cool thought but would it happen? I seriously doubted it, but it was interesting to imagine.

As soon as the choppers were loaded with all of the gear they called for us and we all began to load. It was a pretty odd looking bunch of troops. All of the 25th ID were twenty-something kids with clean shaven baby faces and uniforms that were perfect, even for a combat zone. The rest of us looked like anti-GI Joes, with thick beards and miss-matched desert camouflage. By this time, we were pretty ragtag. As usual, we all carried extra ammo and were ready for whatever was waiting for us at the supposedly abandoned camp.

As we lifted off I thought to myself, *here we go, off to Al Farouk training camp, home of Al Qaeda.* The trip only took about forty five minutes and as we approached the landing zone, we all readied ourselves for exiting the aircraft. This was strictly a no frills flight.

No tray tables to be restored to their locked and upright position. No cocktail cups to toss away. As we touched down there was nervous silence and then the ramp hummed as it lowered. The first guys in the lead charged down the ramp and the rest of us followed, spilling out like toy soldiers from a Tonka toy. We all assumed the stance for a cold landing but were ready for a hot one should a welcoming committee be waiting for us.

The big rotor blades were kicking up a thick dust storm and we couldn't see a thing. We fanned out quickly and formed a perimeter and as the dust settled we realized we were alone. That was a good feeling. We also realized that we had been dropped off in the middle of the Garmaback Gar mountain range and we had it all to ourselves. If we did get hit out here, once the helos had lifted off, there would be nobody to help us. We were not just alone, we were on our own. We had no vehicles to drive away from here as we had a week earlier in the Hotak raid. As we rallied together and got our bearings, we determined that we had been dropped quite some distance from the camp. It would be a hefty little hike to get there, easily a mile or two. I volunteered to go in the front and lead the way. At least if you're in the lead, you know what's coming, what's going on. You're not stuck in the back waiting on somebody else to tell you what's what.

As we trudged through the high desert to get to our mission point it became apparent very quickly how hot it truly was in Afghanistan. One of the guys said that it hit 127 degrees that day. I would have guessed hotter. No one whined or complained, there was just some good natured joking about being choppered out and dropped in hell, like a bad practical joke.

We traversed across a tall ridgeline and then dropped down through a valley to once again climb up onto the flat area where the camp had once been a hotbed of terrorist training and activity. We moved past the ghostly training grounds that had obviously been used for physical training. Next were the firing ranges and up on the mountainsides we could see the defensive positions that they had built into the sides of the mountain. I recognized a lot of the terrain from the Al Qaeda training videos I had watched back in Virginia. The valley was like a small ancient fortress. Not much of a fortress in today's world. The US bombings had demolished the majority of the camp's buildings and left mostly rubble.

Once we entered the main area of the camp compound, the security force formed a defensive perimeter, while the rest of us discussed the game plan. The planning was stopped when we noticed how poorly Chief looked. I sincerely believed he was suffering from heat exhaustion bordering on being a heat casualty. He was extremely pale and had almost stopped sweating by this point. The walk into camp had been tough on all of us, but apparently for Chief, a crusty old Chief Warrant Officer 4 (CW4), it had proven to be nearly fatal. We quickly built a small shelter out of ponchos to provide him some shade from the blazing hot sun and made sure he drank a lot of water. The last thing we needed was for Chief to go down on this mission.

After getting back to formulating a plan, O'Hara organized us into small teams and we all had our own area of responsibility to clear and document. Each team had been equipped with multiple digital cameras and a camcorder. I was working with Bill, the EOD Captain, and a small team from the 25th ID who were serving as our security force. I didn't feel like this group of kids would really be much help at keeping us all alive if something did go sideways, but I was glad to have them along nonetheless. They were definitely extra guns and bullets if we needed them. Fire power can sometimes trump experience.

Nate and Ted had been assigned the south and west sectors of the camp. They had a lot of defensive positions to document, plus all of the other smaller ancillary training sites we had walked through on the way into the valley. O'Hara and Steve were assigned to search the main section of the camp. That was the section where the mosque had been and most of the videos had been filmed. The stately pillars were the only remaining identifiable parts of the mosque still standing. The barracks where many of the September 11 hijackers had slept were now piles of rubble. I couldn't help but think how great it would have been if those men had been inside the barracks when the bombs fell, instead of long gone.

There were caves in the lower part of the valley that we had seen, and O'Hara and Steve would be assigned to search those caves. Amazingly, they would find a black ski mask just like the terrorists wear in the training footage from the 70's. The things we were finding were like artifacts suitable for display in a museum of evil.

Bill and I believed we had the coolest tasking. We walked toward the north and eastern portion of the camp through the narrow corridor the led up into the mountains. I had only taken a few steps when I almost kicked an unexploded grenade that was just lying on the ground. I thought it was rock at first. The EOD captain came over and confirmed that it was an unexploded grenade and "cautioned" us not to touch it. He earned his pay right there. I thought to myself, *like any of us were going to mess around with a grenade that didn't have a pin and wasn't exploded.*

We moved up the valley into our assigned sector and started our sensitive site exploitation. The living quarters had been completely demolished like everything else in the camp. Most of the mud huts that had provided fairly decent shelter at one time were now piles of rubble, although a few of them did still have partial walls standing.

We knew exactly which hut bin Laden used when he was staying here. It was at the top of a staircase, thus easily identifiable. Yes, that is correct. There was a well-crafted staircase in the middle of the Garmaback Gar mountain range built into the side of the valley. It led from the above-ground hut bin Laden used, down to the cave where he hid below ground. It was absolutely the best staircase that I had seen in Afghanistan. It was perfectly sculpted and looked like it had been put together by a master mason. It was an unbelievable site to see, and it was in the middle of nowhere, a surviving testament to some unknown builder's craftsmanship. There was a haunting quality to seeing a stairway going from nowhere to nowhere.

At the base of the staircase was the cave where bin Laden used to hide. We ventured a little way into the cave but didn't think we had time to explore the entire complex. We could see the weapons ports out of the side of the hills. Al Qaeda could have made one heck of a last stand against Ghengis Khan and his army. Against the American military machine they were powerless and I'm sure many of them died right here in these desolate mountains.

We meticulously photographed and videotaped each and every inch of the camp. This was the basis for the military tribunals and it had to be comprehensive. We wouldn't get another shot to come out here and document this stuff. When we were finished with our section of the camp we headed back to the main encampment. It was close to a mile back to the main section from where we were working and everyone was starting to look rather ragged by now. I was extremely fatigued from hiking up and down the mountain all day and I needed to get back and replenish my water supply. I had already drained two full camelbacks and I wanted more. All of us were sweating out more fluid than we could consume. Dehydration is extremely dangerous in that climate and you have to be constantly aware of it.

When we reached the main encampment, the group had set up a perimeter and called for the choppers to come pick us up. We all tried to find a place in the shade, but ending up just dropping to the ground out of sheer fatigue. I would guess that only about three people were actually able to find a place with shade and one of those places was already taken by Chief. He needed to be there. A few minutes after we returned the EOD Captain began vomiting from heat exposure. He claimed another spot in the shade.

It took several long, hot miserable hours before we lifted off from that godforsaken place and the flight back to Kandahar was very quiet. I think everyone was drained, but we were also overwhelmed with what we had seen. To think that the ground we had walked on and the places we had explored had been occupied by our country's worst enemies, terrorists who had vowed our death, was troubling. The images you could conjure up in your mind were ghostly and disturbing. To see videos, to read a book, or to hear about these training camps is one thing, but to actually see it, smell it, and touch the stones was something else altogether. I'll never forget it.

After landing and disembarking from the choppers we were hoping for rides from the tarmac back to our living quarters, but many of us ended up walking back. A rough ending to a rough day.

Then came Tarnak Farms, which has the most misleading name of any camp we came across. Don't let the name fool you. Don't picture green acres or some pastoral setting.

Without much time to recover, the very next day we started all over again on another mission, only this time we had a convoy and not choppers. We were heading out to Tarnak Farms. You may recall from news reports that Tarnak Farms was the infamous training camp where bin Laden's son had gotten married. It was a huge gathering and the CIA could have circumvented the horrific events of September 11 had President Clinton allowed them to blow up his convoy.

The trip out to the camp was relatively short. We could actually see the base from our camp, so it only took a few minutes to get there. At first I thought it was odd that the US base would be so close to the main Taliban/Al Qaeda training camp, but it actually made perfect sense.

The Taliban had been using the Kandahar airport as their headquarters and when the US military took control of the airport during the invasion it only made sense we would set up shop there as well. Al Qaeda had needed a camp close to the airport so they could fly people in and out of the camps with ease and it allowed them to train even more radical Islamic youths than they could at the more remote training camps that often took days travel time to reach. Airports, like rivers, are magnets for humans, good and bad.

The camp looks like a fortress when you pull up to it. It has mud walls that are twenty feet high. We were greeted by some locals who have actually taken up residence and live in the camp now. They seemed receptive at first but as the day drew on they became more and more hostile, as though they were inhibiting our work.

I was again assigned to work with Bill and we once again had the pleasure of documenting the former living quarters of Osama bin Laden. Just like out at Al Farouk in the mountains, the majority of the huts at Tarnak Farms had been completely destroyed by US bombs. We walked around and methodically took pictures of the huts from all angles and then we tried to walk around and get some shots from the back side. At that point, the local squatters started to go crazy, yelling and waving their arms. We had the interpreter ask them what was wrong. They told him that we shouldn't walk back there because there were booby traps and they didn't want us to get hurt. They said there were also land mines and we could get blown up at any minute. Were they concerned for our well being? At first we were a little apprehensive about going behind the ruined huts, believing that they were telling the truth. After all, we had heard from the 'cheeseburger detainee' that he had personally booby trapped a lot of this camp. Something wasn't right. What were the locals trying to do? Protect us or hide something?

As Bill and I had a private conversation about what we should do next I noticed that the path we were trying to follow had single wheel tracks. If someone could ride a bike or take a wheelbarrow down this path it could surely handle our foot traffic. We made the decision to walk behind the buildings and get as much documented as possible. Everything went off without incident but I was still a little spooked about the reaction of the locals. I was convinced they were trying to hide something. You never know who to believe.

As we were taking video a couple of Apache helicopters flew overhead. They fired off a volley of rockets into the field directly behind the houses we were documenting. We learned later, when asking what the hell had gone on, that this place was sometimes used as a target range for the US troops now. It would have been nice to know that ahead of time, but again, we were only told about our part of the job; what the flyboys did was not our need to know.

I clearly recognized some of the areas of this camp from Al Qaeda training videos, just as I had the other camp. The most obvious area recognizable from the video was the obstacle course that was shown on CNN on a near continuous loop after September 11. I think it was the only Al Qaeda footage they had at the time and it got played over and over and over. I watched a number of not-so-publicly available Al Qaeda training videos showing how to conduct vehicle assassinations or kidnappings. The main area of the camp was a large open space.

There were tracks that clearly showed the remnants of a driving course. We used to joke about the video because they always had a motorcycle stop in front of the target vehicle. In real life, any security detail worth its salt would plow right through a motorcycle and keep going. That just shows the level of thought Al Qaeda used in its training. In some things they were incredibly perceptive. In others they were wildly off target and clueless as to how things actually work. The third area of the camp I recognized from the training videos was the explosives range. They had an area where they practiced bomb making and ordnance. We had specific video and the corroboration of the 'cheeseburger detainee' on this area.

Once we finished documenting our area we headed back to the main entrance and rendezvoused with the rest of the team. A few of the guys still had a building to clear and they were apprehensive about entering it because the 'cheeseburger detainee' had warned them that it had been heavily booby trapped. It turned out that this was a very special building - it was the building from which bin Laden issued his fatwas. There was a wall in the background with a map of the world behind bin Laden as he sat at a table with Ayman Al Zawahiri and Mullah Mohammed Omar on either side of him. This was also some famous footage that was overused by every network news channel in America. Some of the guys would ship pieces of that wall home as souvenirs.

The summary of all the work we had done over those two days was to be completed by O'Hara and Steve Harmon. They had the task of sorting through all of the photos and selecting the ones that were of the greatest value to the tribunals and had the best evidentiary value. It was no small task and they spent months working on the follow up presentation linking September 11 hijackers directly to each of the camps. It was extremely comprehensive and was so well accepted that

O'Hara and Steve were later tasked with returning to Afghanistan and documenting other Al Qaeda training camps such as Derunta. Nate and I would be long gone from Afghanistan by the time those missions took place. We didn't even have time to assist with this information because we had been requested to join the SEALs again as they operated out of Kandahar for the next few weeks as they targeted Roze Khan.

Derunta Training Camp was a very well known Al Qaeda training camp. It was located near Jalalabad in the northeast area of Afghanistan. It is north of the region known as Waziristan, the alleged area where bin Laden is currently believed to be hiding out. Derunta was mainly known for the poison training and experimentation that took place at the camp. There were videos released showing the experimental use of poisons and chemical weapons on dogs that allegedly took place at Derunta. The most famous detainee that was trained at Derunta was Ahmed Ressam, also known as the "Millennium Bomber". He was captured trying to infiltrate the United States prior to the turn of the century and was tasked with a spectacular attack during the millennium celebrations.

A camp that has been disputed as being part of the Al Qaeda network was Khalden. A number of the detainees being held at Guantánamo Bay have stated that the camp was never affiliated with Al Qaeda. It may have started as a non-Al Qaeda camp but it survived the Taliban shutdown of camps and eventually became an Al Qaeda camp. It was bombed for that very reason. Khalden was the primary camp used for training terrorists in defensive operations. Those types of operations were primarily designed to attack occupiers of any Muslim country such as Bosnia, Palestine, Chechnya and Afghanistan. The list of senior level Al Qaeda who attended training here is quite long. It includes Ramsi Yousef from the 1993 World Trade Center bombing, Richard Reid the shoe bomber, Omar Al Farouq head of AQ in SE Asia, Mohammed Atta, from the September 11 hijackers, Zacarias Moussaoui arrested in Minneapolis attending flight training, Ahmed Ressam, the Millennium Bomber, Satam al Suqami, another September 11 hijacker, and Mohamed Moumou. Mohammed Moumou is an interesting case. He was connected to Abu Musab Al Zarqawi who later became the head of Al Qaeda in the war in Iraq. He was leading the Al Qaeda charge for the development and use of chemical and biological weapons in Europe.

I didn't have the privilege of investigating all of the major Al Qaeda training camps, but I saw two of the most prominent and the two where the majority of the September 11 hijackers received training. I wish we had taken the training camps out sooner. I wish the administration in power during the 90's had taken steps to prevent the training of thousands of terrorists. The use of pre-emptive strikes against our enemies has become a negative cliché of sorts since the Bush administration invaded Iraq. Personally, after seeing the extensive network of training camps and fully understanding the scope of their intentions, I think Iraq had enough connections to terrorism and enough terrorist training camps alone to warrant being invaded. After September 11, I don't want to see any more countries harboring terrorists and allowing them to train and hone their skills to later use them against the country I love and served to protect. I would rather risk the international reputation of America to prevent another September 11 from happening. Being passive and just allowing things to 'play out' is no longer good enough. Other countries will still trade goods with us even though we invaded Iraq. America is too powerful of a player in the world economy for anyone to shun us and stop trading with us. We need to remain humble as we play our role on the world stage, but we also need to protect ourselves and the line between humble and strong protection was crossed when we allowed ourselves to be attacked on September 11.

I know that Iraq had nothing to do *directly* with the attacks on September 11. But I also know that Iraq harbored and trained many men with extremist views, not just the men who attacked us. America can never let the situation get that bad again. We can only turn a blind eye to extremism for so long before it strikes out and blackens that eye.

Chapter 18
The Taliban Billy the Kid

Who was he? He just looked like a villager sitting under a tree.
Was he a goat herder? Was he the village guardian just watching out
for people approaching the village? I had just come in line with Nate
and the two Navy SEALs and they were intently watching this guy.
He had to be somebody important. We wouldn't know for sure who
he was until later but the calm before the storm was just about to end.

Roze Khan had been on the target list for two years. Everybody
had tried to get him and he kept getting away. Nobody knew how he
was doing it and it was beginning to frustrate the US military. We
would find out how and we would stop him once and for all. The
SEAL team wanted him badly for the death of Brian. They knew that
the best way to get him was to start targeting his lieutenants and work
their way up the chain, which would eventually lead to him. They had
only run a few preliminary missions when the golden ticket was found.
They wanted a chance to punch that ticket.

Lara Logan, a correspondent from CBS News, showed up one day
with her own security guard, a former Navy SEAL named Jim. I met
Lara Logan for the first time at a party that was being thrown by the
New Zealand Special Forces team that was leaving country. They had
completed their final mission and were putting a few beers back to
celebrate before heading home.

I walked into the tent and immediately noticed her. How could
you miss her? She was the only female surrounded by a bunch of
SEAL team guys and New Zealand Special Forces all trying to get
close enough to smell her perfume. It's amazing the changes that men

go through in a combat zone. You miss the littlest things like the "scent of a woman," to quote Al Pacino. You get so used to all the masculine odors associated with locker rooms, sports, and just plain 'manly' smells, you become immune to it. The heat, physical exertion, and lack of daily showers create an atmosphere of pretty gross proportions. Then when on some rare occasion a woman shows up, smelling clean and feminine, it hits you like a slap in the face.

I asked a few guys who she was because I had never seen her before and she was obviously not a SEAL. I was told she was some television news reporter who would be 'taking up space' on the missions for the next week. They didn't seem all that happy that she would be going out on missions with us because she would have to be protected, but they were sure happy as kids on Christmas morning to have her there that night.

Nate and I hung out on the sidelines and kept to ourselves for a while, just observing the play of the wolves and the lamb, but after a while she migrated over our way. I guess she was curious and wanted to talk to the two heavily bearded guys in civilian clothes, see who we were and what we were all about. We didn't exactly blend very well with the SEAL team. They were all in great shape and my call sign was "lunch box". It wasn't that I was in bad shape by any means, but I was clearly not in the same fitness league as a SEAL.

Regardless of fitness levels, we talked with her for a while and learned all about her having grown up in South Africa and how she got into television. She told us her husband played professional basketball in Europe and was from Iowa. I don't know if she thought we were CIA or DIA but I suspect that she talked with us and felt comfortable because we had wedding rings on. We also didn't hastily take them off and shove them in our pockets and unlike the rest of the crowd that night we didn't hit on her every four seconds. We engaged in adult 'getting to know you' conversation and I think she found that comforting in that environment. It had to be a pretty intimidating environment for a female that far from home and surrounded by alpha males. She even invited us to head up to Kabul and have a steak dinner cooked by the chef in the house where the television crew was staying. We would have definitely taken her up on that but unfortunately we weren't in the country long enough.

Ron from the Document Exploitation (DOCEX) team came over the next day and made a request that we help him out. He was slotted to go out on a mission with a company of infantry from the 25th Infantry Division. He had been double-booked and was actually heading out with a team of guys from the 3rd Special Forces Group and wouldn't be able to make it out with the 25th Infantry Division mission. He asked Ted and I to fill in for him and go out with them on the mission. He brought us over to the briefing tent and introduced us to the commander who was leading the mission. He also gave us an overview of the mission. Essentially the team was going to get dropped off at one end of the Argandhab Valley and walk the entire length of the valley to the other end. The goal was to force any Taliban in the valley to come out of hiding and engage them. The Army calls this type of mission a movement to contact. It means go for a long walk and hope somebody comes out of hiding long enough to shoot at you so you can shoot back. This type of mission reveals enemy strength, hiding places, types of weapons, and often results in diminished enemy numbers. It can also result in troop casualties, but we weren't going to think about that.

Ted and I thought this would be an interesting mission since it was scheduled to last two weeks, and was not just a quick in and out. The teams would be out in the Taliban country for an extended period basically looking for a fight. And they were bound to find one. The mission was scheduled to launch the next evening at 2200 hours. As it turns out, I was also double-booked. The SEAL team had requested that Nate and I accompany them on a mission targeting a mid-level Taliban commander.

In preparation for that mission we all went down to the firing range with the SEALs. The main body of SEALs took the first run through the range and then took off. They ensured that their weapons were still in good working condition and the sights were still in alignment. After they left the fun started. Since the majority of the guys that were left were not SEALs we had the SEALs run us through some shooting drills. Some of the junior non-SEALs that were assigned for the mission had never been through any of the shooting training. The Army, in its infinite wisdom, trains soldiers to shoot out of foxholes or lying in the prone position on the ground. The SEALs taught us that day how to shoot while on the move and how to keep the rounds hitting the target. It was very similar to the shooting lessons I had learned from the 3rd Special Forces team with SSG Smith. Louis was the primary instructor and he used his pistol to give us the finer points on double tapping. Double tapping is the art of putting two quick rounds into the same target.

The first hour on the range was spent simply shooting and getting into our groove. Once we were all up to Louis' standards, he moved us into more advanced drills. We practiced shooting while walking toward a target, moving left and then right, and even shooting a target while backing up. We learned how to keep our balance and switch between weapons. We learned what to do if our M-4 runs out of ammo in the middle of a firefight. We had to know how to quickly drop the empty weapon and draw our pistols to keep the enemy engaged. I had been through all of this before and most of the federal agents practiced these skills on a regular basis. Nonetheless, my shooting skills had to significantly improve that day to meet Louis' tough benchmarks.

I walked down to the far end of the range where the 3rd Special Forces Group (SFG) sniper had set up shop. He was practicing with his sniper rifle. I'd never fired one but it reminded me of a hunting rifle from back home. The big difference was that this one fired a 7.62 round. He gave me some pointers on controlling my breathing. I had been taught all the basic techniques fifteen years earlier in basic training but had never been specially trained as a sniper. I fired off ten rounds and put them all into a grouping the size of a quarter. I was pretty impressed with myself and he laughed at me. He laid down behind the rifle and put the next ten rounds right on top of each other in less than ten seconds. I had taken my time and aimed each round before I squeezed the trigger. He just lay down and fired. I guess that's why he is a trained sniper and I am an Intelligence Officer.

That evening I drove Ted down to drop him off with the 25th ID. He was pretty excited because he and Bill had been trying to get included on one of these missions for a couple of months and until now been unsuccessful in penetrating the infantry units. I had managed to breach that gap for them in less than a week. Now this was his shot to prove his value to the 25th ID and get invited back. The downside was that Ted had contracted a virus and had been taking a bunch of anti-diarrhea medicine just prior to the mission. I felt pretty bad for him and it was even worse that I was supposed to go with him and now I couldn't because of the request for me by the Navy SEAL team.

The next morning I woke up and went straight to the gym. I thought it would be a pretty slow day waiting for some intelligence to come in on the mid-level Taliban Commander the team was going after.

Sometime between 1100 and 1200 hours, Nate came into the tent and said, "Grab your gear, we gotta go." Every time he said that something bad happened.

He explained that we had less than forty minutes to get to the airfield and get on the helicopter. The Navy SEALs weren't about to wait for a couple of strap-hangers (extra guys who tag along onto missions like extra gear strapped onto the outside of a backpack) but luckily we made it with minutes to spare. We literally jumped out of the truck and ran onto the helicopter and were airborne within seconds. I think the helo was actually lifting off before my boot left the ground. I had no idea where we were going or who we were going after at that point, only that it was somebody big. A real high value target. During the flight we took care of minor details like putting kneepads on, putting our gloves on, and making sure we had clean goggles for the dust storm that would envelop us as we exited the helicopter on target. We had rehearsed this a dozen times so we knew what order we had to be in and who went which direction when we landed. It had all been mapped out, like a football play, and everybody knew their position. As always happens though, due to the last minute loading we were all seated in the wrong order. We discussed it on the ride, made some quick changes, and adapted to the situation. As we got closer to the target, we were informed that we were ten minutes out from landing. As is standard procedure before hitting a landing zone, each man yells out ten minutes to let the rest of the team know that we are close. As the phrase "ten minutes" echoed around the helicopter, I wondered if this would be a hot landing. That was something nobody wanted. A hot landing is when you hit the ground under fire and that's when all those rehearsals and hours of training pay huge dividends. That was one of the benefits of working with an outfit like the Navy SEALs, because they didn't miss a detail. They all knew their job and had made damn sure we knew ours.

When we finally landed we exited the chopper at a run, blasting into and through the dust storm created by the rotor blades. We then spread out just like we had rehearsed, and set up to provide a secure perimeter around the village.

I had heard a rumor on the helicopter that we were after the infamous Roze Khan. Roze Khan had become a legendary Taliban commander in the southern regions of Afghanistan. Since the war began it had become very apparent that he had risen through the ranks of the Taliban and become a very powerful commander. He began his rise from a low level thug early in the war and as time went on he became more and more powerful. The coalition troops had been hunting Roze for more than two years. Maybe we would be the ones to get him.

We hadn't been on the ground for more than a minute or two when a call came over the radio that someone was trying to make a run from the village and get over the ridgeline. If whoever it was made the ridgeline, it would have been nearly impossible to catch him. Nate and I and the two Navy SEALs were the closest to the ridgeline and the SEAL Commander gave us the order to pursue the man up the mountainside. We were easily a thousand to twelve-hundred meters away from him, but it was tough to judge the distance going up the side of the mountain. Our saving grace came when the Apache escort dropped flares that caused him to take cover under a tree, the only tree, and try to hide from us. My first thought was that he was just a goat herder who had taken refuge under the tree. He was just the lookout for the village and wasn't anyone important. I thought to myself, *why are we watching this guy?* Then it hit me: this was the target. He had tried to calmly saunter out of the village and get over the ridgeline. It took me a second to process that he hadn't started out under the tree and that the flares were meant to scare him and cause him to take cover. That would slow him down and give us time to catch up. So far, it was working.

We closed the gap to less than a hundred meters -roughly a football field away -and formed a line. As we waited and watched, the assault team had sent a four-wheeler from another landing zone to investigate.

As I sat waiting, I thought about how many times I had joked about being a "trained killer" to my family and friends. It always garnered a good laugh and as I watched the man under the tree through the iron sights on my M-4 my perspective changed. I realized this was no longer a joke. This was not my first firefight and not the first time I had fired my weapon at someone with the intention of killing them, but this time was different. I knew we had this guy outnumbered and it didn't seem like a fair fight. He was cornered and probably feeling desperate and hopeless.

As I struggled internally with what was about to happen, the four-wheeler approached the man under the tree, and he rose to his feet and began to fire at it. Instantly my pity for the man went away. I no longer felt sorry for him that he was outnumbered. I didn't care any longer and I wanted him dead. I wanted him dead for Brian, for September 11th, in the name of freedom, this man needed to die. He knew he was out numbered and made his choice. Now he would pay the price. Choices always have consequences, as I was learning.

Once we relayed that he was firing, the call came back on the radio that we were *"weapons free"* and we all opened fire on him. The first volley of rounds lasted twenty to thirty seconds and we knew he was hit at least once. He went down and we figured he was done.

The SEALs with us started yelling, "CHECK FIRE, CHECK FIRE!"

The two SEALs with us had just seen the other team of SEALs approaching up the mountainside on the four-wheeler.

Then I saw muzzle flashes in our direction and the bullets started to zip by us. He wasn't dead yet! My first instinct had been to find cover until I realized I was next to a couple Navy SEALs. I ducked down for a second and started to go prone as I had been taught but I realized that being prone would be of no help in this terrain. The SEALs already knew this so they were kneeling and firing. I returned to my kneeling posture and starting shooting again. We continued to fire until we no longer saw any muzzle flashes or bullets coming our way. During this volley we probably only fired for fifteen to twenty seconds but it seemed like an hour to me. Adrenaline has a way of slowing down the clock, like a time warp. Seconds seem like hours. I was breathing pretty heavy from the run up the mountain and I was struggling to get a good sight picture. I took a deep breath and tried to calm myself as I fired round after round. I'm pretty sure I hit him at least once during this volley.

Again we stopped firing when the SEALs yelled, "CHECK FIRE, CHECK FIRE!"

I thought he had to be dead for sure this time. How much incoming fire can one man take and survive?

To my surprise, I saw another muzzle flash and the SEALs, Nate and I let out our third volley of bullets toward the flash. This time we didn't stop firing until we saw the four-wheeler approaching his position. He didn't appear to be moving any longer and I couldn't tell how many times he had been hit. By now my adrenaline was pumping but thanks to the training, I was able to remain calm enough to fire just fine. As we moved slowly forward and covered the area between our position and the tree, the SEALs on the four-wheeler slowly approached and confirmed that the man was dead.

As he lay there bullet ridden and dead under that tree, I thought to myself, *what if this is really Roze Khan?* That would be a huge turning point for the coalition in Afghanistan. Every time we take out a senior level Taliban commander it disrupts their entire ability to plan and execute operations. They need to find a new commander to replace him and that can take time. Their communications are not effective and it can take a long time just to get word out. I was filled with a feeling of satisfaction and I wanted to know whether or not we had killed the right guy. All indicators pointed to 'yes' but I needed to know for sure.

A search of his body revealed $10,000 in American money and a stack of Pakistani Rupees that was roughly two inches thick. He was heavily armed with an AK, six grenades and six magazines of ammo. Luckily for us, he apparently ran out of ammo while firing and never got the chance to change magazines. Additionally, we found letters addressed to Roze Khan in the pockets of the dead man. We were 99.99% sure that this was our guy. As the criminal investigation team for the SEALs, it was important for everything to be well documented. We thoroughly documented the body, the site, the situation and all the evidence.

Shortly after our victorious firefight with Roze Khan, the SEALs began the assault proper on the village below us. We provided an over watch and the guys with radios were calling down to the SEALs on the ground telling them what to expect in each compound before they entered it. We could see into every compound below and were relaying that information to the guys before they kicked down the door to each compound. Real time intelligence *before* you kick down the door. What a concept! That's something only seen in video games I thought. It was amazing watching the SEALs clear that village. They operated like a well-oiled machine as they systematically moved from compound to compound, very methodically clearing each one along the way.

A short time later they had begun moving fighting aged men into one compound and needed us to come down and begin cuffing and interrogating them. Nate and I moved down the side of the mountain in a bounding maneuver with Sam, our interpreter, following closely behind. We moved down past an orchard until we saw what appeared to be a well but certainly could have been a weapons cache.

Sam yelled down into the well, "If anyone is hiding in there, come out now because we are going to drop a grenade into this well!"

Nobody came out and we didn't drop a grenade. Sometimes a well is just a well. There was a nasty looking puddle of muddy water very close to the well's opening and we assumed that this little ditch was dug to catch the runoff from the mountain. I can't imagine having to drink water that disgusting.

Sam had been issued a pistol prior to the mission for his own safety. As he approached the entrance to the village, one of the SEALs slowly and very carefully took his pistol and uncocked it. I hadn't noticed before now because I had been concentrating on so much else, but Sam looked extremely nervous and was visibly shaking. I can't imagine what it was like to be an interpreter following the soldiers you were assigned to work with and getting into a firefight at such close range. No wonder he was terrified. Most interpreters are kept out of the mix at a safe distance until they are needed. In this case he didn't have a choice. He had pulled the pistol and was prepared to shoot Roze Khan if he needed to. I was very proud of Sam at that moment, for sticking by us and for being courageous. It couldn't have been easy.

Once in the village, we moved into the compound where the SEALs were holding all of the men. I saw Neal and Mike, Neal's dog, watching over the group of men. Neal looked very relaxed at that moment. Lined up around the outer wall of the compound were approximately twenty to thirty men ranging in age from fifteen to sixty years of age.

I dropped my backpack and Kevlar and threw on my 3rd SF Group baseball cap with an American Flag on the front. I started at the far left and worked my way right. I searched each detainee and made sure they had flex cuffs on. When I was finished, I joined Nate and Louis as they interrogated the prisoners. Each and every prisoner we talked to had never heard of Roze Khan. I found that a bit incredible, maybe even a little humorous.

I moved outside past Frank, who was busy fingerprinting each detainee. He had a field laptop with a fingerprint scanner that he was using. It was amazing to see technology at use in the middle of a tiny village in Afghanistan that looked like the eighteenth century was still in their future. It was a real contrast of civilizations and cultures.

Lara Logan was interviewing some of the senior SEALs about the success of killing a commander such as Roze Khan. They told her all about how it would disrupt the operations of the Taliban and make it much harder for the Taliban to pull off future operations. Nobody mentioned the vengeance factor about Brian. They didn't need to. I felt incredibly satisfied knowing that I had been one of the shooters on the mountainside that day. In reality though, if Roze Khan had surrendered, or even not tried to run away, he would not have been killed. His death was the direct result of his decision to fire on U.S. troops. He was hardcore Taliban and wanted to die fighting, I was glad we granted his wish.

The SEALs on the four-wheeler had brought the body down off the mountain by now and it was lying outside the compound. Nate and I went outside to begin the process of documenting Roze Khan. We pulled DNA samples from his body and took close-up pictures of the gunshot wounds, both entry and exit. We took facial shots as well for positive identification by other sources who knew Khan. The final step was fingerprinting the body. Fingerprinting a dead body sounds like a pretty easy task but it can actually be a pain in the butt. We had to wash off his fingers enough to get an actual fingerprint to show up. When we finished I headed outside the village with a Navy EOD tech to blow up the grenades that we had found on Khan. The CBS cameraman came with us and filmed the explosions. It wasn't nearly as cool as the Hotak explosion but I get a kick out of things blowing up. I must have some redneck blood in me somewhere, or maybe it's just a 'guy' thing.

About the time that we were walking back into the village, a taxi could be seen driving toward us from the valley. Everyone was wondering what a taxi was doing way out here. We would soon find out.

When it reached the village, the SEALs stopped the taxi and pulled the people out from inside. One of the occupants was a young man roughly twenty, that didn't seem to be acting normally. He was immediately flagged and fingerprinted and his fingerprints were run through the database that Frank had access to. They hit. We had a positive match on this kid which meant he had been arrested before.

A further search of the kid turned up a number of documents that were addressed to senior level Taliban. My first suspicion was that this kid was a courier. His job was to travel between villages and deliver letters between the senior commanders and that's how they planned the missions. Remember I told you, their communications systems are pretty primitive. If he had arrived a few hours earlier I think we would have missed our target. I have a feeling that the only reason Khan was still in the village was to wait for the courier to bring him his next set of commands.

We were anxious to get back to base, because we knew we had to interrogate the courier as soon as possible. Louis recognized him from the Ghazni raid where Mohammed Easa had been missed. The kid's lying eyes gave him away. Plus, he told us the same lame story he had told Louis during interrogations two months earlier about how his sister just had a baby and he was coming back from visiting her. I think Louis would have gladly strangled the kid if we had let him. He knew that this kid was connected to the guys who killed Brian. We were glad that Roze Khan was dead because he was the one that ordered the attack, but Easa was the guy who executed the attack.

Before we got down to the intelligence business of analyzing what we had brought back, we spent some time taking photos with Lara Logan.

After returning to Kandahar, we used most of the evening going through the intelligence and prioritizing it, making sure that actionable intelligence was analyzed and forwarded on. I was still working, when around 0200 hours I was summoned to the airfield to pick up Special Agent Bob.

On the drive back to the tent he asked what we had done that day and I explained that we had been on the Roze Khan mission and had been in the firefight that killed Khan. He seemed surprised and remarked that Roze Khan was a low-level thug. Why would we care about him?

I responded that Roze Khan had emerged as the most senior Taliban commander in southern Afghanistan. He laughed and told me I was crazy. I was a bit offended since I had been in country reading the intelligence and working to track this guy down for months. I blew it off and dropped him off at the tent. I headed back to the SEAL compound to continue going through the intelligence. Little did I know that conversation would come back to haunt me in my final days in Afghanistan.

The next day I spent all day in the booth with the courier talking with him about his family and his "new" niece, who later somehow turned into a nephew during course of the questioning. We knew he was lying to us and we needed to find the right approach to break him ASAP. It was an extremely frustrating day of questioning for both me and Ted. One of the counter-interrogation techniques he used was to refuse to drink anything. This was right out of the Al Qaeda manual. They thought that the Americans would force them to drink and then tie their penis off with string so that they couldn't urinate. I don't remember being taught that approach but then I didn't write the Al Qaeda manual. Either way the kid wasn't breaking.

In between analyzing the intelligence and questioning the courier, we made a trip over to the morgue. We pulled Roze Khan's body out of the cooler and we showed it to a local Afghani who had been captured and tortured by Khan. He broke down in tears when we showed him the body. It was an extremely emotional moment for all of us but it was blatantly obvious that this man was very happy that Roze Khan was dead.

We asked the obvious question, "Why?"

The man was a former Afghan soldier and he told us a story about getting captured by Khan and his men and being tortured. He pulled up his pant legs and showed us the scars that covered 90% of his legs. Khan had poured boiling hot oil on the man's legs to torture him for joining forces with the Americans. The man told us that he considered himself the lucky one. Of the twenty men that had been captured, he was the only survivor. The rest of the men had been killed in front of him, many by Khan himself. Khan was trying to get information about

American operations out of them and none of them would talk. There is a reason that we *shouldn't use torture* as a means to obtain information and this just reinforced that for me. The man was released because the villagers had come out and begged for Khan to let him go. They had stood up for him and it had worked. The man's sobbing turned into full fledged crying as he relayed this part of the story because he knew that he was the only one who had survived. He felt the guilt of losing his entire platoon. I can't imagine what that feels like.

Our last ditch effort to break the kid was to bring in an Afghani sergeant major to identify the courier. Louis had recognized him from up near Ghazni and the sergeant major from the unit up there was essential in identifying him. We had briefed him that he was to identify the kid and if necessary yell at him to scare him into talking a bit. The approach we chose to use was a 'fear up'. We thought for sure that we could threaten to release him and tell him that the Afghan troops would pick him up right away. They knew who he was and we would no longer be able to protect him. We offered to provide him security if he talked to us. The approach backfired when as soon as we removed the hood from the kid the Sergeant Major recognized and realized who he was and who he was connected to. He leapt across the table and smacked the kid before any of us knew what was happening. As I have stated, I did not witness any abuse by American troops. We handled prisoners very professionally. I was standing outside the tent with a small group of MP's when the smack took place but we all heard it and knew what had just happened. Almost immediately, Ted walked out of the tent and explained to the MP's what had just happened.

We handled the incident *by the book*. Our moral courage kept us from accepting the situation and enabling it to continue. We all recognized that the situation was not right and we had the moral courage to stop it. We briefed the sergeant major ahead of time and when he crossed the line we stopped him and reported the incident immediately. In the wake of Abu Graib however, that wasn't good enough. Within hours we had our access to the prison, and more importantly the prisoners, revoked and were not allowed to continue to do our jobs. That was just the beginning.

The next day Nate called me and asked if I had told Bob that we shot Khan.

I said, "Yes." I described the mission to him and told him we were on the side of the mountain pumping rounds into Roze Khan. The mission was no secret. By this time it had been reported by Lara Logan on CBS news and was hitting the Associated Press wires. It was all *over* the news, at least for a day.

Nate swore a few times and hung up. I knew, obviously, that he was upset but I didn't know why.

Special Agent Bob was changing our orders, pulling us from supporting the SEALs, and wanted us to return to Bagram Airbase ASAP. We checked on flights and found that we couldn't leave until after midnight. Apparently, getting our access revoked, going on the mission with the SEALs and the fallout from the Hotak mission, as spun by Norbert (our interpreter), was enough for Bob to shut us down. We knew that we had absolutely done nothing wrong and it was very upsetting and disappointing to get called back without finishing the job.

When we arrived at Bagram Airbase around 0300 hours Monday, we were greeted by Bill who drove us back to the compound. Special Agent Bob met us as we were unloading and told us to turn in our weapons and that we were being sent out of the country for an investigation into our "rogue" activity.

Nothing we had done was outside the chain of command and every mission had been cleared by Chief. He knew who we were operating with and the risks involved and we had our marching orders from COL Mallow. We had to endure filling out investigative reports and being interrogated for the next couple days and Nate was sent home on Tuesday. I was to leave the following Tuesday. At this point, I was pretty angry and I wanted to leave right away. If I couldn't do my job then I just wanted to be home. Unfortunately that wouldn't happen.

Special Agent Bob, it seems, wanted to separate Nate and I to keep us from "conspiring to make our stories match". I wasn't worried about that since I knew our stories would match anyway. We had lived through some pretty serious missions, had each other's back many times, and I was confident that our perception of those events was nearly identical.

Chapter 19
Goodbye Afghanistan

On my last night in Afghanistan, Lawrence threw me a going away party. A few days earlier he had thrown one for Nate and now it was my turn in the limelight. Dozens of people showed up which signified to me that I had touched a lot of people during my tour and earned their respect. It was entirely mutual. Bill and Ted came over from our compound. A number of the CIA operatives were present, most of whom I only knew by their first names. I am fairly confident that not even the first names given to us were real.

The Document Exploitation team of Ron and Ken were present. Ron was his usual party-boy self getting wasted on scotch. Ken and I had only worked together very briefly but I must have made a big impression on him. He was a wearing a t-shirt from the 3rd Special Forces Group whom we had both frequently worked with. I made a comment about the t-shirt and that I wanted to get one before I left. The t-shirt had a Harley Davidson symbol on the front but instead of saying Harley Davidson it said "Bush Hogs, 2nd BN 3rd Special Forces Group". The back of the t-shirt also had a Harley feel to it but around the outside of the symbol it said "We do bad things to bad people!" Ken responded that he was given the t-shirt by a buddy of his on one of the A-teams and they were pretty hard to come by. I must have looked extremely disappointed because Ken asked me if I wanted his shirt. I really didn't know if he was serious or not and I wasn't about to accept a t-shirt that had been given to someone else. As it turned out I didn't have a choice. He ran over to the trailer that he was staying in and changed his shirt and brought the 3rd Special Forces

Group t-shirt back out for me. I was truly stunned. Had he really just given me the shirt off his back?

I had an epiphany at that moment that I really had made a difference. I had worked hard enough to impress a lot of people on my tour of Afghanistan but this was the icing on the cake. I had impressed someone so much that they were willing to give me the shirt off their back. I felt an enormous surge of pride and gratitude at that moment.

I still wasn't sure how to respond so I merely said a completely inadequate, "Thank you." Ken was another one of the intelligence professionals who will forever remain nameless but who has given so much for this country. I was proud to have worked with him. I still have the shirt and treasure it.

Corporal K and his sidekick, the dip shit marine, came out as well. They had proved their worth many times over in the targeting cell. Manuel Ramirez and his boss were there as well. The list goes on and on and I realized that I had actually enjoyed some pretty good times working with a lot of smart, dedicated people.

The traditional hair cutting and beard shaving ceremony began around 2300 hours and commenced with 1st Lieutenant Stephanie Martin, an intelligence officer from the 25th ID sitting on my lap and whacking a big strip of hair off my beard. Nate and I had worked with her a lot during our tour and she had become a good friend. All of the rest of the females then took turns with the clippers, as Lawrence had arranged, and with each turn my appearance began to transform as they took off big chunks of hair. I hadn't realized how much hair I had grown during my tour. It only took a few minutes, though, for it all to be in a pile on the floor. Bill stepped in when we ran out of females and cleaned up my head, trimming me up so I wouldn't look like a homeless guy on the trip home. I would assume that most of the girls hadn't ever used a set of clippers before and it showed. Bill on the other hand was experienced, and used them back in the Ranger Battalion.

Most of the people from that night have moved on and I don't have contact with them anymore. Many of them have left the intelligence community altogether and are now safely home as civilians much like myself. I travel to Washington, DC periodically and I try to call them when I get out there but I don't always have time to arrange get-togethers. Many of them are still actively involved in the Global War on Terror and have deployed to various places around the world. I suspect that I won't see many of them ever again.

Chapter 20
Interrogating my Morals and Integrity!

I knew the trip back to Washington DC would be a long and lonely one. Instead of traveling back on the Attorney General's G-5 as I had arranged with the FBI, I was now being sent home on a transport plane like the rest of the soldiers. I had worked my heart out for eight months only to have someone question my integrity and basically kick me out of the country.

As I waited at the airfield and then went through customs, feeling cooler, cleaner and lighter than I had in many months, I couldn't help but chuckle as I thought about Erika, Mary and Josh trying to get through customs a couple months earlier. I hadn't heard anything about the fallout from customs finding the porn in their bags but I am sure it was an embarrassing moment for them. I had taken the liberty of shipping most of my gear home the day before so I only had a backpack and my rifle case. It cost me extra to ship it but to skip the hassle of loading and accounting for a couple duffle bags and hard cases full of gear was well worth it. I had learned that lesson when I came home from Bosnia in 1999.

I boarded a C-5 cargo plane and claimed a seat in the back of the plane. I was still in civilian clothes so none of the other soldiers would talk with me. I had shaved my beard the night before in the CIA compound so I wasn't quite as scary looking but they still ignored me.

I arrived in Germany the next day and spent one night there before I was able to jump on a commercial flight back to the states. Most of the poor troops I had been traveling with so far had been sent to the military flight line to await transport back to the states. I would be flying as a civilian. I enjoyed a few beers that night and woke up early the next morning to check my rifle out of the armory so I could catch my flight. This was the same rifle that I had fired back at Ft. Benning, took three tries to qualify with, and then never fired once in Afghanistan. It was a major pain to be transporting a weapon I didn't need.

When I arrived at the airport in Newark, I opened the cell phone that hadn't been turned on for over eight months, praying the battery still worked. I was in luck and the first number I called was my wife's. She was crying when she answered the phone because she knew that using my cell phone meant I was back in the United States. It was an incredibly emotional feeling for me and I am sure for her as well. We only talked for a few minutes but she knew I was home safe and I would get to see her very soon. I proceeded through customs and boarded my flight to Baltimore Airport. I was one step closer to home.

I called the office when I landed in Baltimore and let them know that I needed a ride. I had sent them an email the night before and let them know what time my flight would be arriving but I didn't have a lot of faith that they would have someone waiting for me when I arrived. As I suspected, they weren't waiting and I had to sit at the airport for a few hours until someone arrived to pick me up. Disappointing but at least I was nearly home.

For the next four days, I spent my time going in and out of the warehouse as it was still called, and meeting with federal agents. Special Agent Bob had actually opened three separate investigations into our activity. It was beginning to look like he was on his own mission to destroy our credibility and reputations. He would fail.

I was interrogated about the Hotak mission, the Afghani sergeant major slapping incident, and even being a shooter on the Khan mission. Talk about turning the tables, I couldn't believe what was happening. I had just spent eight months of my life putting it on the line only to have my dignity snatched away and trampled on by Special Agent Bob.

I cooperated fully, knowing that I had followed procedures in each and every situation and I had always followed my moral compass. I knew that I had made the right choices and I was confident the investigators would eventually conclude the same.

All three investigations found that we had done nothing wrong.

In fact, Nate was awarded the Distinguished Civilian Service Award, which is the highest honor awarded for civilians serving in the U.S. Navy. I was awarded a Bronze Star Medal for my service through the Hotak mission, not surprising, I received nothing for the Khan mission. I heard a rumor (never confirmed though) that the two Seals on that hillside were also awarded Bronze Stars with a V device for Valor. They deserved it!

Interrogation of Morals / 226

Chapter 21
Adjusting to Civilian Life

I think one of the hardest aspects of being a citizen soldier as opposed to a fulltime career soldier is having to transition back to being a civilian. Especially with the repeated deployments many reserve troops experience, the back and forth readjustments are brutal. Any of the thousands of soldiers who have fought in the Global War on Terror since it began in 2001 can attest to and confirm this scenario. There are many feelings and emotions to deal with. Sometimes anger, sometimes sorrow, sometimes grief, it all depends on the day. Sometimes I miss the adrenaline rush. Sometimes it's the camaraderie I miss. Not a day goes by that I don't envision pulling the trigger. I pulled the trigger multiple times but I can't get the vision of the last time out of my head. Watching Roze Khan fall to the ground and breathe his last breath sits in my head. I see it every day. I don't regret it for one minute because I know it was the right thing to do, but in our culture we value life. Taking one is not done lightly. After hearing the stories of the atrocities that Khan caused, I feel no guilt over his death. But absence of guilt or not, I can still picture him falling over as if it just happened.

For the first few months after I returned I simply didn't want to deal with people. I didn't seem to have anything in common with anyone, at least not what I was now feeling. When you are serving in the military, it's like living in a separate universe and everyone around you is going through the same thing. You have that common bond, even though they are from a different part of the country, are doing a different job, and you have nothing else in common. Once back in the civilian world, you are around people who have never shot anyone, have never been in danger of dying, and have probably never even fired a weapon. They also most certainly have never been face-to-face with a brutal terrorist, who if given half a chance would slit your throat.

I even had a hard time talking to my wife. I didn't know how to talk about what I had been through, what I had done, or the things I had seen. How much would she want to hear? Was I sharing, or burdening her? How much was too much? I wanted to express what I felt and why I felt it but I just couldn't do it.

I was fortunate enough to have all sorts of friends and neighbors who wanted to come see me and until that moment I hadn't realized how many people were affected by what I had done - serving in the military in a war zone. It is humbling to have people thank you for your service. I still don't know how to respond when someone thanks me for going to Afghanistan. It always makes me feel uncomfortable and embarrassed, but I know they mean well and I am truly grateful for their appreciation. It's just hard to express.

To kill the time, I finished my basement. I had never done a big home improvement project like that before and I wanted to prove to myself that I wasn't losing my mind. That I could still keep it together. The work kept me busy and kept my mind off the experiences that I was trying to forget. Busy hands and all that. It was healing to focus on building something and doing something positive.

I felt a genuine lack of trust and I was certain that everyone was out to get me. I thought that everyone was talking about me and I got the feeling that people were avoiding me as I walked the halls of Retek. I felt as if nobody would talk to me. Even worse, I thought that people were afraid to ask me questions. That's probably because when they did I got very defensive. I suddenly didn't know how to communicate with people as I had always done in the past. I used to be the guy that everyone asked to do presentations and talk to management groups. I didn't feel like I could do that anymore.

I was feeling a genuine lack of confidence which was odd considering what I had just lived through. *I doubted every decision I made at work and I thought everyone would notice when I made a mistake. I was lost and I didn't want anyone to know it.* I had just left the environment where a mistake meant someone could be killed and now I was afraid to make a mistake on a PowerPoint presentation or a spread sheet.

I began applying for different jobs in anticipation of getting fired for being incompetent. I thought I would end up screwing up a major account or saying something ridiculous to the wrong executive. Then on my birthday the unthinkable happened. I showed up for work that morning ready to give my notice. I was ready to accept a job I had interviewed for and had even set up a chunk of stock options to be sold at the opening bell. The price jumped over $3 that day and I pulled the trigger to sell the stock. I thought I had pulled off a great coup along with giving myself a wonderful birthday present and began preparing my resignation letter.

Not until later that morning did I realize what was happening to the company. Another major software company had placed a bid to buy out the company. A week later another company overbid them and they entered a bidding war. I had lost a fair chunk of cash by selling my company stock prematurely, and this only cemented my feelings of incompetence.

I held on to my resignation letter, but as time went on and the acquisition started to take effect I didn't know what I should do. I had an opportunity to cash out and walk away for a while. I chose to stick it out and try out the new company for a while.

Over the next few months, I butted heads with my new boss. I asked for a promotion that I had no business getting and he knew it. He was a complete jerk about it but he knew it wasn't the right time for me to move up. He didn't know me or my background because he had joined the company during my deployment. He always threw out military and war references in his speeches and it really bugged me. Every time he said we need to "kill the competition" and referred to them as "the enemy" it was like a knife being twisted in my back. I thought to myself that this sales guy has no idea what it is like to actually kill the enemy. It drove me nuts.

Eventually I gave up and took a position with another company. That only lasted about five months before I changed jobs again. Each time I changed jobs I took one with responsibilities that I had never done before to prove to myself that I could do it. I was engaged in a constant battle with myself to prove that I could actually do something.

As I began to research Post Traumatic Stress Disorder, I figured out this is somewhat normal behavior. I was beating myself up and I didn't know why. The only thing that worked for me was to start writing. I wrote a lot of stories and articles explaining various positions on the war and torture and I always ended up deleting them. I didn't want anyone to know that I had those thoughts in my head.

There are a number of excellent programs that have been developed since the Global War on Terror began. Most of them are the result of a veteran seeing a need to help another veteran and having the moral courage to act and make a difference. One of those programs was designed by the Minnesota National Guard. The program is called "Beyond the Yellow Ribbon". It assists soldiers who have recently returned from a war zone by giving them guidance and helping them to reintegrate into society. Operating in a war zone is entirely different than working in a cubicle in corporate America.

The "Beyond the Yellow Ribbon" program has been incredibly successful for Minnesota veterans and is being used as a model for returning soldiers nationwide.

My life has settled down a lot since my return home but I still struggle every day. Most of my family, friends and coworkers have no idea about my internal struggles and to be honest, I don't want them to know. Some days are worse than others but each day gets easier as time goes on.

My basement was finished and my next project was to start a family. In April of 2007, my wife and I welcomed a beautiful little girl named Samantha into our lives. I thank God every day for the wonderful life I have and the opportunities that I am blessed with by living in America. When I look at Samantha I can't help but think about the little girl who spoke to me in Afghanistan and the opportunity to go to school and learn and grow up in a free country. I know the situation in Afghanistan is not perfect but all we can do is leave the place better than when we arrived. I have no doubt in my mind that our Courage and Integrity has afforded others in the world the same opportunities that I was born with.

"for in truth Lies victory"

§

Afterword
Broken Partisan Politics

I wasted a lot of time watching TV after I resumed my civilian life and the majority of the stories were in response to some political pundit on TV claiming that the work I had been engaged in was worthless and we should pull out today. The election of 2004 had just ended and presidential candidate John Kerry had made a theme in his campaign that this was "the wrong war at the wrong time". I knew he had to have been looking at the same intelligence that I was while I was in Afghanistan and I didn't understand how he came to that conclusion. He was a member of the Senate Intelligence Committee and yet he was claiming things in his campaign that I knew were blatantly false about the war in Iraq. Sentiment turned it from the War on Terror to the War in Iraq. The two fronts were becoming disconnected as the war began to politicize. I knew I had to get more involved.

To be honest, I didn't know the difference between a Democrat and a Republican when I decided to get involved. All throughout the Bosnia conflict I watched the Republicans play the same games that the Democrats were now playing. Threatening to cut off funding and *"end this unjust war."* Many Republicans were notably outspoken regarding the bombing campaign and occupation of Kosovo. It would seem that the Democrats had raided the playbook in 2004 and were using the same tactics to undermine President Bush as he led us into conflicts in Afghanistan and Iraq. Both of those conflicts had been voted on and overwhelmingly approved by Congress and now

Congress was failing to support the troops. Rather than take responsibility for the war they blamed it on President Bush.

Obviously with perfect hindsight, many mistakes were made and there were many areas where improvement was necessary for us to be successful in Iraq. Those areas were recognized and adjustments were made. Our military knows how to react and adjust when necessary and made recommendations to our civilian leadership. It took some time to accept the failures but eventually the adjustments were made and the troops got what they needed. American soldiers can win wars if the politicians can stop being politicians and support the troops.

I started to attend meetings on both sides of the aisle. In my naïve little mind I thought I should run for Congress to change the government and clean it up. I was frustrated by the rhetoric and the never-ending blaming that goes back and forth between the parties. Isn't the government set up to represent the people, not the political parties?

The Democratic meetings I attended weren't really very enjoyable. It truly was a group of bitter people getting together to complain about the "Republicans". They didn't offer any solutions to problems, only to defeat the other side. I sent an email to the commissioner of the congressional district I lived in and told him I was interested in exploring a run for Congress. He told me to show up at the next meeting and he would give me some information. When I showed up at the meeting I felt like I was ambushed because he threw me to the crowd in the room and told them to ask me whatever they wanted because I was a Congressional candidate. I was baffled. I had literally asked for information on how to become a candidate and that got turned into my being a candidate.

During the meeting I got grilled about everything from why we were fighting an unjust and immoral war to questions about the illegality of the Patriot Act. I responded as I thought appropriate and I soon realized that I was not a Democrat. The final straw was when one of the gentlemen asked for the district to pay his way down to a conference in Kansas City so he could learn how to put "spin" on information so they could compete with the Republicans. I asked the guys I shared the table with why they would need to do that. Isn't the truth something that should be communicated without any spin? They wanted to learn how to deliberately misconstrue information for their purposes. I'm not naïve enough to think that spin doesn't happen on both sides of the aisle but to have classes and educate the entire party how to spin rhetoric was more than I could handle. I realize that every Democrat that reads this will counter with the tired old line that both sides use: "They did it first!"

I was extremely turned off by the disorganization, anger and the bickering that took place at the Democrat meeting. I decided I needed to check out the Republican side of the aisle as well. I sent an email to my State Representative and asked him how I could get involved with the Republican Party in my area. I included a short biography of my background. Being a recently returned veteran, small business owner, and family man I felt the information was extremely relevant. He responded very quickly with contact information for my local Basic Political Organization Unit (BPOU) and told me to contact his uncle. I promptly did so and attended the next meeting.

When I walked into the meeting I was greeted by a gentleman who introduced himself and it turns out he was the uncle of my State Representative. He immediately knew who I was and proceeded to introduce me to the rest of the people in the meeting. I found out that he was the Vice Chair of the BPOU and knowing him has become a great asset for me. I felt genuinely accepted right from the start. There is no bickering at the Republican meetings. Republicans know what they stand for and it's easy for them to unite. I don't always agree with the alienation of Republicans who stray from the strict party line but on the same note it keeps the party together and on the same page. The same cannot be said for the Democrats. They are all over the board with stances and I doubt they will ever come to a consensus. The lone exception being to dislike Republicans.

If I had political aspirations I thought it would be a tough call for me to determine which party to align with. I clearly fall into the conservative Republican category but if you cross party lines and work with the Democrats across the aisle you get eaten by your own party for straying and accused of not having "values". Democrats on the other hand have few real stances on any one issue and therefore it is easy to cross party lines to partner with the other side and actually get something accomplished. Is it better to toe the line as a staunch Republican or be billed as a "Moderate" Democrat and accomplish a lot more by working with the Republicans?

It took me a few years to come to a conclusion regarding the difference between being a Democrat and a Republican. I viewed them all as politicians. Today I can tell you honestly that I am an American, first and foremost. As I stood up for veterans and allowed my voice to be heard in support of my brethren who were *still fighting* in Iraq and Afghanistan, I had a revelation about where I stood and how I got there. I was standing up for something that I believed in. My moral compass had led me to this place. I want my elected officials to stand for what they believe in rather than what the party believes in. Each member of Congress should be voting their own conscience with each and every vote. They should never be voting strictly down the party line. That bears repeating. Politicians need to follow a moral compass and not a party line. I want people to know who I am and what I stand for. I am an American who believes in protecting our rights, freedoms and liberties just as my forefathers have for over two centuries. America should always come before the party. I am definitely conservative and fall in line with the right side of the political spectrum but I don't want that to define me. I want people to know that I am an American.

As of June 2008 the President's approval rating was at 29%. Not even 1 out of 3 people think he is doing a good job. As much as this upsets me, he is only one man. Congress had an approval rating of 19%. That's less than 1 out 5 people think Congress is doing a good job. 535 members in Congress and Americans only think 101 of them are doing a satisfactory job. How can this be? Shouldn't we expect the opposite to be true? I want to see 4 out of 5 Americans approve of the job Congress is doing. In the current state of long term politicians and partisan politics I don't see an end in sight. In order for that approval rating to rise, politicians need to have the interests of Americans in mind, not reelection. They need to work together to make decisions for America, not prevent each other from achieving their "agenda". Collaboration on both sides of the aisle is what will earn the trust of American citizens because that's when citizens will start to see results being produced.

Most important, they need to determine which direction their own personal moral compass points and follow it. It is easy to stand on the sidelines and point out mistakes without ever getting into the game. It's another thing to experience the battle and be faced with making the difficult decisions. Following your moral compass becomes imperative.

A *political* battle is raging in America right now and the combatants have lost sight of what is important. They focus on the topic of the day for political gain, be it the high gas prices, war casualties, the housing market collapse or even the deficit. The Right is using soldiers to fight wars, which is our job. That is how we should be used.

The Left is using soldiers for political gain. I am disgusted by the misinformation campaign regarding the American soldier. The left and the media have portrayed the American soldier as a bunch of raping, murdering, torturing, cold blooded killers. When they aren't positioning us as the cruel heartless type they are trying to paint us as victims. All this when they should be supporting us so we can finish the job that Congress and the President sent us to do.

Soldiers are neither. They are people trained to do a job and that job is to kill the enemy if necessary in order to protect the citizens of America. We are not victims of this war. We are selfless volunteers and as such we should be taken care of for our sacrifice. That does not make us victims and should not be spun as such. In a world where so many people feel they are "entitled" to things rather than having to work for them, I find it comforting that the ultimate selfless servants, our soldiers, are not rising up and claiming a stake in America. That's because we understand that it takes the sacrifices that we are making, above all else, for the country to remain free.

I wrote this book about my experience fighting in the Global War on Terror and that experience culminated with an investigation that questioned my very integrity which ultimately led to my resignation from the US Army. An overzealous Army CID agent opened investigations of alleged abuse. One was ignited by our interpreter who had witnessed my partner, an NCIS agent, subdue a detainee that was trying to resist. He used standard law enforcement tactics to take the man down and hold him on the ground. Another incident involved the Afghan Sergeant Major (SGM) who was brought in to identify a prisoner and when he recognized the prisoner he smacked him pretty good. We had immediately restrained the Afghan SGM and reported the incident through the military police. In the wake of Abu Ghraib it didn't matter and even those actions were questioned and investigated. *I let my honor and integrity speak for itself.* I told the truth and the allegations were cleared because we had done nothing wrong. As a country we fall prey to the media hype that typically accompanies anything perceived as wrong. The good deeds that we perform get glossed over or flat out ignored because the doom and gloom is deemed more important.

The Criminal Investigation task force had the ominous task of sorting through the detainees captured in the Global War on Terror. We had an entire section dedicated to the initial screenings of detainees and made determinations on the level of terror suspect or determined they were not related to terror. We had advanced cells that investigated terrorists who funneled money, the terrorists that trained new recruits and bodyguards for the Al Qaeda leadership. Federal agents and intelligence professionals dedicated to keeping only the terrorists and releasing the innocent detainees.

Federal agents worked tirelessly for months and years researching and investigating the detainees at Guantanamo Bay. They coordinated with the CIA, INTERPOL, FBI, Secret Service and anyone else who had information about these men. The reality was some of them did not have the evidence chain necessary for our civilian judicial system. They had literally been rounded up on the battlefield and as such there wasn't evidence collected against them. Senior level Al Qaeda operatives were captured throughout the world in areas that did not allow a crime scene investigation that we would expect in America. This is not a law enforcement action, this is a military action in a time of war. The left wants law enforcement and the right wants military action, I believe it has to be military action. *We must always remember we are fighting for freedom and liberty, not Democrats or Republicans.*

The most important aspect, above all else, is preserving our freedom and liberties. Without them we won't have the luxury of going to the mall or owning a home. If we lose sight of the foundation that America was built upon then we have lost already. Our forefathers recognized that we had an opportunity, let me say that again, *an opportunity* to establish something great. A country where everyone has the opportunity to be successful! It is important for our elected leadership to recognize and honor that concept. America offers opportunity and nothing more. It is up to each individual to take advantage of that opportunity.

In the private sector when the leadership is performing poorly, they are quickly and decisively removed. In the government world of elected officials they are elected, or not, by the people, which is a slow and often unresponsive system. In the military the removal is even quicker. Leadership skills are necessary to survive in the military. Politicians know that the path to keeping their job is to spin everything they do as a positive. Only during scandals do career politicians get removed from office. So how do we make a change?

I want this book to touch, move and inspire people to take a long hard look at themselves, what they do every day, and make responsible changes that will benefit America. Gone are the days of the individual, because America is much bigger than one single person. People need to be accountable for themselves and that will make the country as a whole much better. I live in the *United* States of America. All the individuals make up the collective citizens of our great country.

America is the ship that enables the voyage but individual responsibility is the key that keeps it from sinking. The crew should be steering the ship to the destination that passengers desire. Lately, it seems the crew is only going in the direction the crew wants to go. As government grows, it's like adding anchors to the ship that prevents it from going anywhere. The balance here is maintaining individual sovereignty and getting the country back on the right track. There is no simple answer other than it will take everyone stepping up and taking responsibility for their own little piece of the ship and removing the anchors. If everyone is responsible for themselves the entire country will be better off. *For the collective good of America, we need the citizens of America to be individually responsible.* Our government was not implemented as a caretaker for the country. It was founded in such a way as to leave the people alone to live their lives in whatever means they choose as long as it doesn't harm others. I believe it is really that simple. *So how do we motivate people to take care of their own business and not expect the government to handle it for them?*

My vision for America is to inspire as many military veterans as possible to become active and involved in our government. Our system of government was set up by the founding fathers for self-regulation and self-correction which are necessary to fight corruption. In America, a revolution does not need to take place with guns and riots, although we are guaranteed the right to bear arms in case our government does become oppressive or unresponsive.

The revolution in America can take place with the action of the people. Our government is meant to be "of the people, by the people, and for the people". It only takes a small group of motivated people to create momentum and grow into a powerful force. That small group can vote themselves into the positions of the decision makers for either party (or better yet, both of them) by getting elected as delegates in the system. The delegates are the ones who choose the platform of the party and the candidates for the party. Not the people during elections, *the delegates prior to the election.* That's where the real power in this country lies and that's where the power can be grasped by Americans and taken back from the career politicians and their cronies who have corrupted our current system. Currently, all of their efforts are being spent raising money and trying to stay in office and creating political power through the use of public funds for what should be private ventures.

Veterans are the one group in this country who know the true meaning of selfless service, courage, integrity, and patriotism. They have placed themselves in harm's way and put their lives on the line for the freedom and liberty that America provides. There is nothing more noble than that. Veterans embody the courage and integrity that this country needs to remain the great country that our forefathers founded.

I believe that courage is the ability to confront wrongdoing even when the odds are against you. Courage is being afraid and still finding the ability to act. Courage is knowing that you may not come back, but you go anyway. Courage is the heart and soul of every Veteran who has laid down his or her life for freedom.

Integrity is doing what you know is right. Integrity is keeping your commitments even when times get tough. Integrity is knowing when you have broken a commitment and having the moral fortitude to make a new commitment. Integrity belongs in the heart of every American. It should be the hallmark of our government leaders, but too often it is missing in action.

Veterans understand selfless service more than any other segment of the population. We understand what it means to put the greater good of the country ahead of your own well being. Politicians believe they are serving constituents but I don't think many of them truly understand what that means. As a soldier I understand that America is bigger than any one person, including me. I believe that protecting and preserving America is more important than any one soldier's life, including mine. Without America and all she stands for, that life will be lost anyway. Some things are worth sacrificing for and America is at the top of the list.

Everyone has a moral compass but most people don't realize it or know how or when to use it. A moral compass is the internal thought process that points us toward right or wrong. It can be formed and transformed many times in one's life. As a person grows older that compass seems like it becomes more involved and more complex but in actuality it becomes simpler and easier to understand. Knowing how to determine when a situation or action is right or wrong becomes easy. Soldiers get tested on their moral compass every day when they are in a war zone. Having the integrity to follow your own moral compass takes courage.

Veterans can be the savior of this country. They have the discipline to correct themselves when they make a mistake. They keep each other in line and they know the price of failure. The proud and loyal veterans of this country have fought in wars since the very beginning of America. They know how to make the right decisions both morally and ethically. They know that making the wrong decision can cost people dearly. America has trusted its future to a group of career politicians.

The citizens can change that by using the system as it was designed and getting many more of our veterans into the system. By demonstrating the courage and integrity that I believed in while I fought to protect the country I love, I found my moral compass.

Our future lies in the courage and integrity of our veterans.

§

~Acknowledgements_____

I couldn't have written this book without the support and sometimes aggressive prompting of my wife Karen. Karen thank you for always being there when I returned home, I love you.

To my family who has always supported me, thank you. Mom and Dad, you have always been an inspiration to me and I owe you more than I can ever repay. I learned my morals and values from watching you as I grew into the man I am today, thank you. To my sister, Toni who endured a year of hell while Dean was deployed, you have always been my role model and advisor, thank you. Tom and Bob, I appreciate all of your support and for always being there when I need you.

To Greg and Paula, Thank you for the support. Greg, special thanks to you for convincing me to go fishing in Canada. I accomplished so much on this book up there it was amazing. The huge fish were a bonus.

I need to thank JoAnn Mathews who gave me a ton of advice and happens to be the sister of my mother in law and an accomplished writer herself. Her editing, knowledge of the industry and suggestions were invaluable. Pat Barnhart did an incredible job of editing the book for me from cover to cover. Thank you both, I couldn't have done it without you.

The book wouldn't have existed without the men and women I served with in Afghanistan and Washington DC. Thank you all.

Notes

1. http://www.fas.org/irp/doddir/army/fm3-24fd.pdf
2. http://www.nationaldefensemagazine.org/issues/2008/February/U.S
3. http://findarticles.com/p/articles/mi_m0PAJ/is_6_55/ai_11248212
4. http://www.defenselink.mil/privacy/notices/army/A0195-2c_USACID
5. http://www.wood.army.mil/mpbulletin/pdfs/Spring%2007%20pdfs/Powlen.pdf
6. http://english.aljazeera.net/News/aspx/print.htm
7. http://www.arlingtoncemetery.net/beprice.htm
8. http://www.defenselink.mil/news/Mar2005/d20050304info.pdf
9. http://www.defenselink.mil/news/d20080613Returntothefightfactsheet.pdf
10. http://en.wikipedia.org/wiki/United_States_Navy_Special_Warfare_Development_Group
11. Ibid.
12. http://feedlot.blogspot.com/2005/11/developing-omar-al-faruq-wa
13. http://www.globalsecurity.org/security/profiles/omar_al-farouq.
14. http://www.specialoperations.com/Navy/SEALs/st2.html
15. http://www.rferl.org/featuresarticleprint/2005/06/20e43cc0-156f
16. http://english.aljazeera.net/News/aspx/print.htm
17. http://www.worldpress.org/asia/0202tempo.htm
18. http://www.military.com/NewsContent/0,13319,FL_taliban_071904,00.html

About the Author

Jason Meszaros was a Captain in the US Army Reserve and deployed to Afghanistan in 2004. He served as an Intelligence Officer and operated mostly in the Special Operations Community. During his decade of service he conducted intelligence operations in multiple theaters in the Global War on Terror. While in Afghanistan Meszaros was assigned to several task forces and his work and the work of others led to capture of several senior Al Qaeda and Taliban operatives.

He is currently the Chief Information Officer for a n agency in the state of MN. He is also the Director of Operations for the Minnesota Chapter of Vets for Freedom (www.vetsforfreedom.org)

He currently resides in Minnesota with his wife, Karen and daughter, Samantha.